MEMOIR

OF

JOSIAH WHITE.

SHOWING HIS CONNECTION WITH THE INTRODUCTION AND USE OF ANTHRACITE COAL AND IRON, AND THE CONSTRUCTION OF SOME OF THE CANALS AND RAILROADS OF PENNSYLVANIA, ETC.

BY RICHARD RICHARDSON.

PHILADELPHIA:
J. B. LIPPINCOTT & CO.
1873.

LIPPINCOTT'S PRESS,
PHILADELPHIA.

Josiah White.

PREFACE.

In the preparation of the following memoir of Josiah White, it has been the object of the writer to endeavor not only to portray the life of the individual as a man and a Christian, illustrating how energy and industry, with strict integrity of character, by the blessing of Providence, meet with their sure reward; which has been verified in the history of most of our prominent men in all professions of life, who have been the architects of their own fortunes; but also chiefly to depict some of the difficulties he had to encounter, as a pioneer, in the successful development of the vast mineral resources of our State, in which he took a leading and active part.

The extensive system of internal improvements by canal and railroad, with their adjuncts of motive-power and telegraphs, and other extensive works connected therewith, now so important and necessary to the industry and traffic of the country, and so familiar to the public, ought not to allow us to forget the men, who originated and inaugurated what may now be considered the humble beginnings of these things. These beginnings, in reality, required much more originality of thought, courage, and energy to carry through to success than many larger enterprises of the present day, when capital is so abundant, and mechanical appliances are so perfect and so readily obtained.

As the name of De Witt Clinton, in New York, stands pre-eminent as the pioneer of the canal system of that State, so must that of Josiah White be conspicuous, in the same direction, in the State of Pennsylvania. They were both remarkable men in their day, and occupied marked positions in the history of the growth and development of the wealth and enterprise of these great Commonwealths.

The anthracite coal in this country being almost exclusively confined to Pennsylvania, as far as developed, has become a leading article of its mineral wealth; its mining, transportation, and introduction into the markets of the State and country, formed the basis of Josiah White's operations, and gave him scope and opportunity to fully display the patience, perseverance, and skill which were distinguishing features in his character. The manufacture of iron with anthracite coal, another leading article in our productions, also claimed his attention, and he, in connection with some others, were among the first who succeeded in making and introducing it into use.

As regards his religious tenets, he was thoughtfully inclined from his youth, regularly attending the meetings of the Society of Friends, of which he was a member, and was much interested in its prosperity and welfare. In an essay written towards the close of his life, this language occurs, illustrative of his religious feelings: "I am now beyond the meridian of life, and have been busied with temporal engagements, I hope honestly and for the advantage of my country and fellow-creatures. I now seek and pray for retirement from all these, so as to understand the realities I stand in need of in regard to another world." His daily life, with his frequent seasons of solitary retirement, with the Bible for his companion, which he diligently read and studied, were well known to his family; the earnestness of his resolution to keep his face Zionward, desiring to be at peace with his Maker, through a once crucified, but now risen and glorified Saviour, is attested by the few extracts presented to the reader in this little volume.

In some of the copious quotations from his writings presented in this work occasional verbal alterations have been made, but not so as to impair the meaning intended to be conveyed by him.

The writer feeling his incompetency for the task he has undertaken, that of giving a faithful portraiture of his esteemed and honored father-in-law, submits it, with all its imperfections, to the lenient criticism of the reader. R. R.

PHILADELPHIA, 1873.

CONTENTS.

BIRTHPLACE OF JOSIAH WHITE, COR. OF WHITE AND PINE STS., MT. HOLLY, N. J.

MEMOIR

OF

JOSIAH WHITE.

CHAPTER I.

EARLY LIFE.

THE subject of this memoir, Josiah White, was born at Mount Holly, in Burlington County, State of New Jersey, on the 4th of the 3d month, 1781. He was the son of John and Rebecca White, members of the Society of Friends, residing at that place.

He was directly descended from Thomas White, of Omnen, Cumberland County, England; whose son, Christopher White, with his wife Elizabeth, with two sons, appear to have emigrated to America in the year 1677. Christopher White had previously to his emigration purchased of John Fenwick, one of the proprietors of the then province of New Jersey, one thousand acres of land, on Alloway's Creek, near Salem, in that State. He erected on his farm one of the first brick dwellings constructed in Salem County, and the largest at that time, the bricks being imported from England. It remained standing until so recently as about the year 1855.

Christopher White had a son, Josiah White, born in London, England, in 1675, whose son, Josiah White, born in 1705, was the grandfather of the Josiah White of this memoir.

His mother, Rebecca Haines, was of English descent, traced back to William and Sarah Haines of the seventeenth century.

John White, the father, pursued the business of fulling cloth, having a mill for that and other purposes at Mount Holly, on Rancocus Creek; he was also to some extent a farmer, owning a landed estate in the vicinity. The business had been established by his father, Josiah White, who removed from Salem County, after losing much of his property in an attempt to dam Alloway's Creek, for the purpose of reclaiming land overflowed by the tide. When the dam was nearly completed it was secretly and maliciously destroyed, by cutting a passage for the water through it, whereby it was speedily washed away, and he lost the remuneration he was to have received upon the completion of the undertaking.

John White, for whom his son retained a feeling of veneration, and of whom in after-life he frequently spoke in terms of affection and regard, was taken from him by death, when at an early age; leaving his mother, whom he calls a "widow indeed," with the care of four young sons, of whom he was the third.

She continued her husband's business in the same place for a time, bringing up her children in a reputable manner, training them in habits of industry and economy; setting them the example herself.

The schools at that period afforded but poor facilities for an extended literary education; the teachers being many of them ignorant foreign adventurers, poorly paid, and having little or no capacity for conveying to others the small amount of knowledge they possessed. Such facilities as the place afforded in this respect he enjoyed whilst he remained at Mount Holly; but his school education was limited and defective, being the occasion of many regrets to him in after-life. He says, in alluding to this: "During my fourteenth year I saw the utility of education, and felt a pleasure the first time in my life in learning; previous to which I thought that play, such as boys had, was that which gave the greatest enjoyment to life, and that education was not of much account; and I dreaded the period when I should arrive at manhood, feeling that something more useful would be required of me. My schoolmasters, instead of impressing on their scholars the advantages of knowledge by reason and argument, used the rod as the stimulant to learning, telling us we must 'either get our lessons or it;' thereby frequently causing what ought to have been a pleasure to become a physical pain to us, and discouraging a proper attempt at learning." Had suitable opportunities been afforded in this respect,—judging from the natural force, native talent, and determination of his character,—but little difficulty would have been experienced by him in mastering any literary or scientific subject that might have claimed his attention. A more scientific knowledge of the principles of mechanics would often have saved him a vast amount of trouble and expense in his future pursuits. This was one of the principal causes, I believe, why he generally trusted more to his perceptive than to his reasoning faculties in the construction of the various machinery, etc., which he invented and made. It was seldom that a clear idea was conveyed to his mind merely by a written description of anything of the kind; it must be seen by his eyes to be thoroughly understood, by means of a draft or model; and a model was always preferred if practicable. "*I want to see if it will go*," was his usual expression on such occasions.

He left Mount Holly at an early age to enter into business, but ever after retained vivid recollections of his juvenile life whilst residing there; and was in the habit of frequently visiting the place of his nativity in his advanced life, going to the points where some remarkable event occurred; the old swimming and skating places on the creek, where he and his brothers enjoyed their boyish sports and dangerous adventures; spots where more serious occurrences took place, the breaking of an arm, the cut from an axe, or the fall into the creek and narrow escape from drowning; here he made hay, there the spring of water where he reposed and partook of luncheon; here grew the chestnut-tree, commemorative of a remarkable dream; all these places, and the room where he was born, the school-house in which he was educated, the meeting-house where he worshiped, and the grave-yard where reposed the ashes of his ancestors, he would visit and revisit, with untiring interest and pleasure.

About the fifteenth year of his age he was apprenticed to James Hutton, of Philadelphia. Of this he says: "My mother took me to Philadelphia to get me apprenticed to some business there; she urged no trade in particular, but had inculcated into her children a dislike to store-keeping, as too much encouraging pride and idleness, and rather tending to a cunning craftiness, that she was fearful might be disadvantageous to us. I preferred a mechanical trade, a joiner or carpenter, as I was fond of tools." They spent a day, unsuccessfully, looking for a situation. On stating to his uncle,

Daniel Drinker, the next day their want of success, he informed them that a friend of his in the hardware business needed a boy, and undertook to introduce him. On his way there he says: "I began to reflect that I might be too quick in agreeing to enter a business that might not answer the purpose I had in view, that of making a living, and that if it did not, I had better stay at home. I immediately asked my uncle if it was a business I could make a living by, and money at, after I was of age, and if it was respectable, and his friend a well-disposed man. He replied to all my questions in the affirmative, said that it was the same business he had followed. This satisfied me, (as my uncle had been prosperous and was reputed rich,) that I could gain a living by it in an honest way. I accordingly proceeded with him to his friend, James Hutton, on the north side of Market Street, between Front and Second Streets, who kept a small hardware store, who at once engaged me, agreeing to board and pay me twenty dollars a year."

At the end of two years he had most of the business to attend to, including the keeping of the books. He says: "By the time I was twenty years of age, I became dissatisfied, and thought I had better learn another trade, as this was too small a business for me; but this project was soon stopped, as my employer asked five hundred dollars for the last year of my time, which I thought I could not afford to pay. It is true I was not bound, or legally required to stay with him, nor had ever agreed to; he told me at first to let him know in two or three weeks if I was satisfied, but neither of us ever adverted to the subject again; but I felt the implication quite strong enough to bind me, as a measure of duty, and remained with him, which conclusion was no doubt of after-use to me, as it tended to keep me settled. About eighteen months before I was twenty-one years of age, I was sent to Maiden Creek, to take an account of the stock of store-goods my employer had in partnership with another person at that place. This was about seventy miles from Philadelphia, and the first time I had been over forty miles from home."

Before he was twenty-one years of age he sold his patrimonial estate, and purchased the hardware stock of Joseph Dilworth, No. 111 Market Street, who was then retiring therefrom. He proceeds: "My estate amounted to between five and six thousand dollars. The old stock of goods was about one thousand dollars, and I ordered about five thousand dollars' worth from England, to arrive the spring I was of age, and four thousand dollars more for the fall trade."

He entered into the hardware business on his own account on the day after he was of age, on the 5th of the 3d month, 1802, "intending" he says, "not to lose a day until I had made as much as I thought was enough, (which was forty thousand dollars,) provided I had attained that amount before I was thirty years old. If I was successful, to then put twenty thousand dollars at interest to accumulate eight times, as I expected in thirty-six years, and to live on the other twenty thousand dollars in such way as I chose. I proposed buying a farm for eight or ten thousand dollars, and with this and eight to ten thousand dollars at interest to live on, to make me as nearly independent of all necessary business, and calls from all quarters, as in the nature of things and the will of Providence I could be. I gave up promptly all my predilections for mechanics of all kinds, for fear they would grow on me to the prejudice of my business, being fully persuaded that the most agreeable way of getting along with any business was to lay aside all things that interfered with it, and make it a strong point *to endeavor to like whatever business* I judged was necessary for me, and then, after making enough, to leave it *in toto.*"

Diligence in business and economy were ruling traits in his character at all times, but particularly so during his continuance in trade on Market Street. He made his place of business his residence, and led an abstemious and industrious life, marked by integrity and probity.

He was married to Catharine Ridgway, of New Jersey, in 1805, in his twenty-fifth year. This connection was, however, of short continuance. His wife died of pulmonary disease in less than three years. After this event, his mother was induced to live with her son, and take charge of his domestic arrangements.

He continues his narrative: "About the twenty-eighth year of my age, I sold out my goods to my brother, Joseph White, and Samuel Lippincott; having by this time obtained the amount of property I had desired, as being sufficient for me. My aim had been to lose no time until I had acquired enough; and then, to appropriate the balance of the life a good Providence allowed me in such a way as would give me the most comfort. No morning, I thought, ever opened more clearly than mine now presented, having realized by industry and integrity my best anticipations, escaped the pollutions of trade, having an abiding feeling to do what was right in the sight of my Maker and fellow-man; with a desire to be useful to the latter, and to do what was strictly right in the eyes of the former; with good hopes to rely on for a peaceful, pleasant, and moderate progress through life, so as to step from a calm journey, through this world, into that which never ends.

"During the two years I was out of business, I made a tour to Georgia by sea, and returned by land. I was invited by Barrack Gibbons to accompany him to his river plantation, near Savannah. Having just returned home from the North, his slaves received him as kindly as though he was a near friend. I concluded the slaveholders had something to gratify their pride, in contrasting themselves with their slaves; but that their comforts were much fewer than those in the North, with the same wealth; and that northern labor was cheaper than theirs, considering the large proportion of useless and indifferent laborers, and the small amount of work done by the best hands; all having to be supported at a cost, as I estimated it, of forty dollars each per annum. In the large cities, and in some places in the country, they were obliged to have patrols at night, for fear of a rising among the blacks. On the average, one hundred slaves turn out about one-third, or thirty-three per cent., prime hands; the others being either too young, too old, too lazy, or sick."

On his return home, he says: "I looked for a good farm, with a small water-power, to aid me; the farm I intended to afford me an independent living; expecting to raise maple-trees, make my own sugar, and all other necessaries of life that were possible; and felt ambitious to pursue a plan of business and life that would serve as a pattern to others in comfort and independence."

In the renewal of a youthful affection, he sought

and obtained, in marriage, in 1810, Elizabeth, the daughter of Solomon and Hannah White; her father had been a respectable and successful merchant of Philadelphia, then deceased. Their city residence was in Arch Street, between Seventh and Eighth Streets, and for a summer home they had a country seat of three acres of land, on Ridge Avenue, above Callowhill Street, called "Rural Hall." In these days, it is amusing to imagine the country so near, and also the shortness of the drive in going from one to the other of their homes. The newly-married pair established themselves with the widowed parent in the city. It is believed the country seat was abandoned as a residence after the death of Solomon White; Josiah White having engaged in business at the Falls of Schuylkill, the family found it more convenient, as well as agreeable, to live a portion of the year in that suburban village, returning to the ancestral home at any time when they desired to enjoy its privileges. It was the birthplace of their five children.

CHAPTER II.

RESIDENCE AT THE FALLS OF SCHUYLKILL.

NOTWITHSTANDING all these resolutions and plans of life, he was destined to enter deeper than he had ever yet experienced into the vortex of trade, and the vicissitudes and perplexities of a troublesome water-power and manufacturing business. But we will hear his own account of the beginning of his future activity: "About two years having elapsed since I declined business in Market Street, a water-power was offered for sale at the 'Falls of Schuylkill,' belonging to Robert Kennedy, comprising three and a half or four feet of available fall, with all the water of the river, with the right to construct a lock for navigation, charging fifty cents toll on each boat for passing; also, three or four acres of ground on the east side, and seven or eight acres, and an old tavern house, on the west side of the river, adjoining the bridge.* Here was an improvement to

* "On the 9th April, 1807, Mr. Robert Kennedy, an enterprising gentleman then occupying the Falls Hotel, obtained, from the Legislature of Pennsylvania, an act vesting in him the right of the water-power at the Falls, on the condition of building locks for

be made by dams and locks, to produce a large water-power near to Philadelphia, but it would require money, perseverance, and ingenuity to carry it through. It occurred to me that this might be a providential opening towards carrying out my arranged plan of life; and, if I succeeded, it might lead to similar useful improvements in the interior of the State, which might be of great public good. No public improvement of this kind had as yet succeeded in Pennsylvania.

"The Schuylkill had not yet been dammed, neither had any locks in the State ever succeeded, excepting two at York Haven, on the Susquehanna. The Susquehanna, Schuylkill, and Union Canals had failed, and were given up. The city of Philadelphia was supplied with water by steam-power, there being at that time no faith in making any permanent dams in so large a stream. Here, I thought, was a choice offered between applying my means and talents in a way that might be of singular use to my fellow-beings, and would not impair

the accommodation of boats then plying on the river."—Early History of the Falls of Schuylkill, etc., by Charles V. Hagner. He was authorized by this act "to dig, continue, support, and keep in repair a mill-race, on and contiguous to said tract of land, to extend a certain distance into the Schuylkill River as should be necessary for a grist- or saw-mill, or such other machinery as it should by him be found expedient to establish, according to the provisions, limitations, and conditions in the said act of General Assembly mentioned."

my estate, and without involving me in much trouble. On the other hand, I could invest my money, do nothing for others, and pass down the hill of life without good or harm, and also be free from care and trouble. I also thought, I might have been blessed thus early in life with the means and the ability for the execution of this great work, especially as I believed I had discovered a peculiar plan of constructing dams that would insure their permanency.

"I finally concluded to purchase the property, which I did in the spring of 1810."

The falls in the Schuylkill River were caused by an irregular barrier of rocks, extending across the stream in a diagonal direction; these rocks were of unequal height and prominence, over and through which the water effected its course, boiling and foaming as it went, forming a waterfall or rapid at ordinary times of about six or seven feet in height, and one hundred to two hundred yards in length, and when the river was swollen, of greater altitude. This place was then a picturesque and rural spot, much frequented for its beauty, and for fishing and other aquatic sports.

The navigation at that time was by the natural channel of the river. Charles V. Hagner, in his "History of the Falls," remarks of the boats that navigated the river, that they "were long and narrow, sharp at both ends, and carrying from seventy-five to one hundred and fifty barrels of flour. They were generally manned with five men, and were only used in freshets or high water. They required five men, not for bringing them down,—for they drifted down rapidly with the current,—but to take them back; which was done by the use of poles shod with iron, and was very hard work; of course they could take no return cargoes. It was an exciting and beautiful sight to see these boats descending the falls, which they did with great rapidity. Sometimes they would be almost lost to sight, and the next instant mounted high on the waves; in some instances they were wrecked."

The plan Josiah White adopted to make the water-power available, and at the same time to improve the navigation of the river, was by closing the interstices of the rocks, and so connecting their prominences as to render the obstruction more complete and continuous, leaving a sufficient channel open in the centre for the free passage of downward boats; on the western side to make a channel or canal three or four hundred yards, with a side wall, or bank, on the river-side, with entrance and outlet locks, by which the navigation was effected round the falls; from which also the water could be drawn for manufacturing purposes. On the eastern side were guard-walls and a race-way to convey the water to the mills on that side. These improvements involved a large amount of ingenuity and money, as well as hard work, and required more than eleven hundred feet of dams and side walls, and the building of strong and substantial locks and head-gates, etc., etc.; in a large river often subject to violent freshets of great volumes of water, and floating ice; with little experience or information to be gained from other sources to guide him.* The locks were eighty feet long and seventeen feet wide. His original idea appears to have been, after making the water-power available, to let it out to others for a consideration, the amount of water to be disposed of in this way being great.

He soon found that his purchase was not likely to meet his expectations. He says: "I had supposed the necessary improvements to make the property productive, and the expense, would be within my means; but I soon discovered my error, and instead of being the man of leisure I had expected, I must, to secure myself from ruin, leave all my mechanical amusements, and turn in to the roughest and most exposed parts of the business. In cold weather I labored up to my breast in water

---

* "The winters, it seems to me, were longer and colder; and before the present succession of dams were made in the river the ice came down in immensely large fields, with great momentum, and sometimes as much as from two to three feet thick. It seemed to me that nothing could resist its force."—Hagner's History of the Falls.

to raise stone out of the channel; and had in reality to say to my workmen, '*Come, boys,*' in the place of '*Go, boys,*' as I had expected.

"My efforts, from 1810 to 1818 to improve my estate so as to make it productive in the shape of renting water-power, proved futile; there was a prejudice against the property as a mere rental estate, and another difficulty arose from the liability to frequent delays from back-water. Independently of my being a party and holding an interest in the rental, I could induce no business to come there."

The plan of renting water-power, which he states there was "prejudice against," has since then become quite common in various parts of the United States, and on this river but two miles above this point, at Manayunk, the Schuylkill Navigation Company derive a large revenue from renting water-power for manufacturing purposes; so that may we not attribute its failure to a lack of manufacturing spirit in the country at that time, more than to any prejudice against it, as he supposed? In reality, it appears to have been a premature effort, in advance of the times.

He built a large mill for the manufacture of wire and a smaller one for making nails, and entered himself into the manufacture of these articles. Here his first business acquaintance with Erskine Hazard commenced, who was afterwards associated with him in the improvement of the Lehigh River. They were in partnership in the manufacture of wire. At that time no well-constructed machinery was in use for either of these purposes, and he was obliged to exert his inventive faculties to produce something for the purpose. He took out a patent in 1810 for rolling iron, nails, etc., and in 1812 others for the same purpose, and for making wire and heading nails. The state of the mechanic arts at this time was such, that many an ingenious inventor was foiled in expected results, from inability to procure suitable machinery for carrying into use the conceptions of his brain, and the failures were attributed to the defectiveness of the plan, rather than to the real cause, the defects in the machine. From this cause, John Fitch failed successfully to navigate the Delaware River by steam, and Oliver Evans severely felt the want. The difficulties and embarrassments, resulting therefrom, can scarcely be appreciated at this day, when most kinds of machinery are so readily and so completely constructed. As it was, Josiah White had not only to invent, but also to make the machinery, and the very tools used in its fabrication.

"Whether," he continues, "my decision to purchase the 'Falls' property was a correct or an incorrect course I must leave. I certainly endeavored to feel for the best direction, and do not think I was moved by any caprice or carelessness in the conclusion. It introduced me into a sea of trouble and disappointment, from which I was entirely unable to extricate myself with propriety for seven years. For although we succeeded in making wire and wrought rolled nails, and essentially succeeded in every branch of business which we undertook, so far as to perfect the articles, yet none proved profitable; and in addition our mills were both burned down, and had to be rebuilt or the business be abandoned." He sold the small mill and seven-sixteenths of his interest in the water-power to Joseph Gillingham; and, afterwards, he and Erskine Hazard joined together and procured a charter from the Legislature of Pennsylvania, in 1816, with a capital of two hundred thousand dollars, by the name of the "Whitestown Manufacturing Co.," for the manufacture of wire, etc., and to enable them to make available the water-power on the western side of the river. The privileges under this charter were, however, never brought into use.

"In the year 1817, Joseph Gillingham and myself made the strongest efforts in our power to make an arrangement with the city of Philadelphia, to supply them with water at Fairmount. We examined the shores of the river down to Callowhill Street, and across the river in several places; one, where the dam now stands, and at nearly opposite Pratt's House. We then offered to supply the city, with three millions of gallons of water every twenty-four hours, for twenty years, for twenty-five thousand dollars a year, and then three millions of gallons every twenty-four hours, at three thousand dollars a year forever; to be paid for in certificates of city loan to make the improvement, they to give us all the city property there, and below the bridge, and the engine and fixtures at Fairmount. This would afford us room to use our surplus water below the dam. By this plan we expected to produce an income of from twenty-five to thirty thousand dollars a year, and what we obtained from the city would enable us to make the whole improvement, and erect the mills for renting, or perfect the site so as to be able to rent them; with the proviso, that the Schuylkill Navigation Company would allow us to use any place on the river to make our dam, above Callowhill Street bridge."

Thus we see his sagacious mind conceived the plan of supplying the city with water, that has since been successfully adopted; and he and his coadjutor were willing to take the risk of carrying it into effect; so certain were they of being able to accomplish it. The subject was for a long time a matter of discussion between them and a committee of the City Councils appointed for the purpose of investigating the project.

At the same time Josiah White wrote a number of essays on the subject, which were published in the papers of the day, setting forth the public advantages of the plan proposed. After several months of negotiation the matter came to an end, the objections urged against it being the uncertainty of the power, in consequence of freshets and backwater, and the impossibility of building a dam in the river that would be permanent; and, also, the unwillingness of the Schuylkill Navigation Company to allow the dam to be made, without what was considered an exorbitant compensation. Fresh negotiations for the sale of their right to the water-power at the "Falls," were, however, entered into, some time afterwards, which resulted in its being purchased by the city in the year 1819, on terms advantageous to the proprietors.

Although his efforts in a business point of view at this place were unsuccessful, yet the experience gained in building dams and locks, and the management of water, and the play it gave to his inventive genius, were of great subsequent use to him and Erskine Hazard, in the greater and more important work of making the navigation on the Lehigh.

They endeavored to induce the public to apply wire to many purposes for which it is now extensively used, such as fencing, bridges, etc. He published several essays on its importance for fencing, showing its durability and cheapness as compared with wood; and they built a wire bridge over the Schuylkill, to test its practicability for that purpose. It was intended for pedestrians only, and mainly for the accommodation of their own workmen, but was considered a great curiosity at the time, and was visited and crossed by hundreds. "This bridge was four hundred feet span, with about thirty-three feet curve, the main wires three-eighths of an inch rolled iron. One ton weight was suspended by one main wire, and it sustained forty persons at one time." They also made and used an iron boat.

CHAPTER III.

EARLY OPERATIONS ON THE LEHIGH.

THE introduction of anthracite coal as a fuel in this country, now so immense in its proportions, commenced not much over fifty years ago. It was slow in being appreciated by the community, and it required vigorous exertions to induce persons to attempt its use. Its appearance was against it,—so different from ordinary fuel,—and many were entirely incredulous as to its being anything else than a stone, and incapable of being burned by any inherent quality of its own. Josiah White and Erskine Hazard had their attention first directed to its use while operating at the Falls of Schuylkill, and their minds impressed with its importance as a fuel. Having procured a small amount from the Lehigh, brought to market by the early operators on that river, one of the first experiments in burning it for manufacturing purposes was made at their works. Incredible as it may appear at the present day, when millions of tons are annually consumed, great difficulty was found in the ignition of it, mainly from deficient draft and want of patience in the management of it.

Erskine Hazard, in a communication published in the proceedings of the Pennsylvania Historical Society, makes this statement.

"During the war (1812), Virginia coal became very scarce, and Messrs. White & Hazard, (who were then manufacturing wire at the Falls of Schuylkill,) having been told by Mr. Joshua Malin that he had succeeded in making use of Lehigh coal in his rolling-mill, procured a cart-load of it, which cost them one dollar per bushel. This quantity was entirely wasted without getting up the requisite heat. Another cart-load was, however, obtained, and a whole night spent in endeavoring to make a fire in the furnace, when the hands shut the furnace-door and left the mill in despair. Fortunately, one of them left his jacket in the mill, and, returning for it in about half an hour, noticed that the door was red-hot, and upon opening it was surprised to find the whole furnace of a glowing white heat. The others were summoned, and four separate parcels of iron were heated and rolled by the same fire before it required renewing. The furnace was then replenished, and, as *letting it alone* had succeeded so well, it was concluded to try it again, and the experiment was repeated with the same result."*

---

* Hagner, in his "History of the Falls of Schuylkill," after describing the process of making the coal burn by White & Hazard,

C. G. Childs, "On the Coal and Iron Trade in 1847," says:

"During the war with Great Britain, bituminous coal rose to high prices. The demand for coal in Philadelphia led Mr. Miner and Mr. Cist to contrive a plan for mining and transporting the Mauch Chunk coal. On the 9th of August, 1814, they started off their first ark from Mauch Chunk (from where Mauch Chunk afterwards was). In less than eighty rods from the place of starting, the ark struck on a ledge and broke a hole in her bow. The lads stripped themselves nearly naked, to stop the rush of water with their clothes. In six days, however, the ark reached Philadelphia with its twenty-four tons of coal, which had by this time cost fourteen dollars a ton. 'But,' says Mr. Miner, 'we had the greatest difficulty to overcome in inducing the public to use our coal when brought to our doors.'"

It was from this cargo, probably, that White & Hazard procured their coal mentioned above.

Coal was known to exist in large quantities near the head waters of the Schuylkill River, and they procured some from there; but the price was "enormously high, forty dollars a ton," brought to their works in wagons. They formed the con-

---

says: "Here was an important discovery, and it was in my opinion the first *practically* successful use of our anthracite coal."

clusion to apply to the legislature to grant them the privilege of making the Schuylkill navigable, so as to bring the coal to market, and supply their own wants at a cheaper rate.

The application was made in 1812–13; but the idea of using coal as a fuel was ridiculed there, and the member from Schuylkill County affirmed in the legislature, "that although they had a black stone in their county, it would not burn." They were unsuccessful; but this, however, was the beginning of movements for a law for that purpose, finally granted to other parties.

The following, from an article by Erskine Hazard, is here quoted from "Hazard's Register," vol. iii., p. 302:

"The application to the legislature, by White & Hazard, as individuals, having failed, they called a meeting of those interested in that navigation, at the tavern, corner of Fifth and Race Streets, Philadelphia, when Mr. White opened the business of the meeting by proposing the application to the legislature for a charter for a company to improve the Schuylkill for slack-water navigation by dams and locks. This was the commencement of the present Schuylkill Navigation Company, which was incorporated in 1815."

Having failed to procure coal for the use of their works at the falls from the Schuylkill region, on reasonable terms, either by a law for the improvement of that river, or, afterwards, from the Navigation Company, to whom they applied for the temporary use of the river, before their work was begun, they turned their attention to the Lehigh region for that purpose.*

From a memoir of Dr. T. C. James, published by the Historical Society of Pennsylvania, is copied an account of the first discovery of coal on the Lehigh by Philip Ginter. It described a journey in that region in 1804, and after stating several difficulties encountered, says:

"In the course of our pilgrimage we reached the summit of Mauch Chunk Mountain, the present site of the mine, or rather quarry, of anthracite coal; at that time there were only to be seen three or four small pits, which had much the appearance of the commencement of rude wells, into one of which our guide descended with great

* "Josiah White about that time started and originated the Schuylkill Navigation Company, which was chartered March 8, 1815. This was another of the beneficial acts of Josiah White, but mark how shabbily he was treated. He was one of the commissioners named in the act of incorporation. He was the father of the whole concern, and if they had hunted Pennsylvania through they could not at that time have found a better man for their purpose; yet, notwithstanding all this, at the first election held at Norristown, they refused to elect him one of the managers, on the flimsy ground that he was interested at the Falls of Schuylkill; but we shall see the consequence of this directly."—Hagner's History of the Falls of Schuylkill, page 45.

ease, and threw up some pieces of coal for our examination; after which, whilst we lingered on the spot, contemplating the wildness of the scene, honest Philip amused us with the following narrative of the original discovery of this most valuable of minerals, now promising, from its general diffusion, so much of wealth and comfort to a great portion of Pennsylvania. When he first took up his residence in that district of country, he built for himself a rough cabin in the forest, and supported himself by the proceeds of his rifle, being literally a hunter of the backwoods. At the particular time to which he then alluded, he was without a supply of food for his family, and after being out all day with his gun, in quest of it, he was returning towards evening over the Mauch Chunk Mountain, unsuccessful and dispirited, in a drizzling rain, and night approaching. As he trod slowly over the ground, his foot stumbled against something, which, by the stroke, was driven before him; observing it to be *black*, to distinguish which there was just light enough remaining, he took it up, and as he had often listened to the traditions of the country of the existence of coal in the vicinity, it occurred to him that this perhaps might be a portion of that '*stone coal*' of which he had heard. He accordingly carefully took it with him to his cabin, and the next day carried it to Colonel Jacob Weiss, residing at what was then known by the name of 'Fort Allen.'* The colonel, who was alive to the subject, brought the specimen with him to Philadelphia and submitted it to the inspection of John Nicholson and Michael Hillegas, Esq., and Charles Cist, an intelligent painter, who ascertained its nature and qualities, and authorized the colonel to satisfy Ginter for his discovery, upon his pointing out the precise spot where he found the coal. This was done by acceding to Ginter's proposition of getting through the forms of the patent-office the title for a small tract of land, which he supposed had never been taken up, containing a mill seat, on which he afterwards built a mill, etc.; and which he was afterwards unhappily deprived of, by the claim of a prior survey.

"Hillegas, Cist, Weiss, and some others immediately, (about the beginning of the year 1792,) formed themselves into what was called the 'Lehigh Coal Mine Company,' but without a charter of incorporation, and took up about eight or ten thousand acres of till then unlocated land, including the Mauch Chunk Mountain, but probably never worked the mine. It remained in this neglected state, being only used by blacksmiths and people in the immediate vicinity, until somewhere about 1806, when Wm. Turnbull, Esq., had an ark con-

* Now Weissport, on the Lehigh, three miles below Mauch Chunk.

structed at Lausanne,* which brought down two or three hundred bushels. This was sold to the managers of the water-works for the use of the Centre Square engine. It was there tried as an experiment, but ultimately rejected as unmanageable; and its character for the time being blasted, the further attempts at introducing it to public notice in this way seemed suspended."

In a communication by Erskine Hazard to the Historical Society, he says:

"In 1792 a company was formed, called the Lehigh Coal Mine Company, who took up a large body of land, contiguous to that on which the coal had been found. They opened the mine where it is at present worked, made a very rough road from the river to the mine, and attempted to bring the coal in arks to the city, in which they but partially succeeded, in consequence of the difficulties of the navigation. A small quantity of coal, however, reached the city; but the want of knowledge of the proper fixtures for its use, together with the difficulties of the navigation, caused the company to abandon their undertaking. Some of the coal, it is said, was tried under the boiler of the engine at the Centre Square, but only served *to put the fire out*, and the remainder was broken up and spread on the walks instead of gravel."

---

* On the Lehigh River, about one mile above Mauch Chunk.

"The legislature was early aware of the importance of the navigation of the Lehigh, and in 1771 passed a law for its improvement. Subsequent laws, for the same object, were enacted in 1791, 1794, 1798, 1810, 1814, and 1816. A company was formed under one of them, which expended upwards of thirty thousand dollars in clearing out channels; one of which they attempted to make through the ledges of slate which extend across the river, about seven miles above Allentown; but they found the slate too hard to pick, and too shelly to blow; and at length considered it an insuperable obstacle to the completion of the work, and relinquished it.

"The Coal Mine Company, in the mean while, anxious to have their property brought into notice, gave leases of their mines to different individuals in succession, for a period of twenty-one, fourteen, and ten years, adding to the last the privilege of taking timber from the lands for the purpose of floating the coal to market. Messrs. Cist, Miner & Robinson, who had the last lease, started several arks, only three of which reached the city, and they abandoned their business at the close of the war, 1815."

Josiah White says: "I had made inquiry into the ownership and condition of the Lehigh mines and river, and determined to visit them and see if anything could be done there. George F. A. Hauto, who was in the practice of occasionally visiting us at the falls to talk about machinery, etc., I told of my intention of visiting the Lehigh on a tour of inspection, and he proposed accompanying me, having had a previous intention of visiting the Schuylkill mines. My stonemason, William Brigs, wanted a ride, and he also concluded to go with us; so we three went on horseback, and got to Bethlehem on Christmas-eve, 1817. We stayed at Lausanne and Lehighton, as the places nearest to the mines, where we could board whilst visiting them, which occupied about a week, one being eleven and the other twelve miles distant from the mine.

"Upon returning home with favorable impressions of the practicability of the project, (of improving the river and mining coal,) it was concluded that Erskine Hazard, George F. A. Hauto,* and myself should join in the enterprise. I was to mature the plan; Hauto was to procure the money from his rich friends; Hazard was to be the scribe, he also being a good machinist and an excellent counselor."

The existence of coal on the Lehigh had been

* This George F. A. Hauto was a German, and had insinuated himself into their confidence by his pretensions to wealth and influence; and who afterwards, when his true character was discovered, had to be bought off at a considerable pecuniary sacrifice.

known for about a quarter of a century previous to this visit; and a company had been formed in the year 1793, called "the Lehigh Coal Mine Company" (before mentioned), who purchased the land upon which the coal was first mined, at Summit Hill, and took up by patent from the State of Pennsylvania other tracts to the extent of ten thousand acres, including nearly all the coal lands now belonging to the Lehigh Coal and Navigation Company, in the first coal-field.

The Lehigh Coal Mine Company made some almost fruitless endeavors to mine and bring the coal to market by their own efforts in the first place, and also by leasing the mine to others; and attempted to make a wagon-road to bring the coal from the mine down to the river, expending the sum of ten pounds, Pennsylvania currency, for the purpose, but soon abandoned the attempt.

In 1813 they leased for ten years their lands to Miner, Cist & Robinson, the consideration being the annual production and transportation to market of ten thousand bushels of coal for the benefit of the lessees. Out of five ark-loads of coal shipped by these parties, two only arrived at Philadelphia, the others having been wrecked on the passage. The most of this coal was bought by White & Hazard for their works at "the Falls" for twenty-one dollars per ton; but even this price was insufficient to remunerate the owners, and consequently the mining and transportation of coal again ceased.

Josiah White continues: "We three at once set about getting a lease of the Lehigh Coal Mine Company's lands, ten thousand acres for twenty years, for *one ear of corn a year*, if demanded; and from and after three years to send to Philadelphia at least forty thousand bushels of coal per annum on our own account, so as to be sure of introducing it into the market, by which means we hoped to make valuable what had heretofore proved to be valueless to the Coal Mine Company; our intention being to procure the property of the mine and river, which by our plan (of navigation) was to support itself. We soon obtained the grant of a lease, as mentioned, which required two or three weeks to perfect, and during this time Erskine Hazard wrote out the law on the principles mentioned, and then we all posted to Harrisburg to procure its passage through the legislature, in which we succeeded on the 20th of March, 1818 (entitled 'An act to improve the navigation of the river Lehigh.')"

He says: "The Lehigh Coal Mine Company had tried to the best of their means to open and work the mine and get the river improved; had a lottery, on which it is said they raised ten thousand dollars, to aid in improving the river. There had been five laws obtained, but all their efforts failed, and the river was abandoned. And it was not until the Lehigh Coal Mine Company—two distinct individual contracts and leases—had failed in working the mines, and also the said five failures in improving the river and denouncing it as impracticable, that we came forward to improve it.

"The plan of improvement I concluded on, (when on my visit,) was the one we subsequently adopted, which was to smooth the old road of nine miles, which the old company had raised ten pounds to make, to get some coal down, to make a noise in Philadelphia, and upon succeeding in raising money, afterwards to make a road of a grade that would ultimately do to lay a railroad upon, with an uninterrupted declivity from the mine to the river. Improve the navigation of the river by contracting the channels funnel fashion, to bring the whole flow of water at each of the falls to as narrow a compass as the law would allow, by throwing up the round river-stones into low walls, not higher than we wanted to raise the water, and if we had not sufficient water for the required depth of fifteen or eighteen inches by the natural flow, to make artificial freshets to supply the deficiency,—that is, by making ponds of water of as many acres as we could get, and letting it off periodically, say once in three days. I supposed we could gather enough water to secure the required quantity, and thus secure a regular *descending* navigation. The plan for locks and gates for letting out the freshet in a proper manner was left for the present to be devised in due time, if found necessary."

They issued a pamphlet entitled "Observations on the Lehigh Navigation Bill" for the information of the members of the legislature, which shows what they proposed to do, from which the following is extracted:

"The improvements in the river Schuylkill, at the falls, by Josiah White & Co., are, we presume, sufficient proof of capability for the undertaking. The dam across that river, the canal and locks, were made and completed by them at their own expense in a few months. The subscribers propose to effect a complete downward navigation for all kinds of boats, arks, crafts, and rafts, and a sufficient upward one, for all and every necessary purpose, by means of dams, canals, locks, wing dams, open sluices, and slopes, clearing and deepening the bed, contracting and straightening the same, and other usual known means, according as circumstances and the nature of the impediment may suggest. Besides, they intend to avail themselves in the driest season (about a month in the year) of artificial freshets."

"In the 4th month, 1818, Erskine Hazard and myself having sat up all night to settle our business at the falls, and giving a power of attorney to another person to attend to the whole of it during our absence, went down to the stage-office to proceed to Stoddartsville (head of the Lehigh), for the purpose of commencing the leveling of the river; but the stage having gone before our arrival proved an advantage, as we were detained a week, the weather becoming milder in the mean time, making it safer and pleasanter to lodge out in the woods. We leveled the river from Stoddartsville to Easton, the ice not having all disappeared; there being no house between the former place and Lausanne obliging us to lie out in the woods for six nights. We borrowed the leveling instruments from Benjamin R. Morgan, who had retained them as the relics of the Union Canal Company: we knew of no others in Philadelphia." The descent from Stoddartsville to Mauch Chunk is nine hundred and twenty-five feet, and from Mauch Chunk to Easton, three hundred and sixty-four feet; distance from Stoddartsville to Easton, eighty-four and a quarter miles.

Above the Gap, in the Blue Mountain, there were but thirteen houses, including the towns of Lausanne and Lehighton, within sight from the river, and for thirty-five miles above Lausanne there was no sign of a human habitation; everything was in a state of nature.

"Having obtained," he continues, "the lease of the mines, our charter for the improvement of the river, and made the survey of the same, we also bought the tract of land on Mauch Chunk Creek, to enable us to make, as we supposed, an unbroken plane for a road, from the large coal bed to the river, (for bringing down the coal,) of two feet in descent in the one hundred feet; but, in laying it out, we discovered that the fall in the creek was too great for two and a half miles of the lower end. We were, therefore, obliged to make a variation in the plan, from one foot to about four and a half feet in the hundred."

The location and survey of this road was made by White and Hazard personally, and is said to have been the first "laid out by an instrument, on the principle of dividing the whole descent into the whole distance, as regularly as the ground would admit of, and have no undulation."

CHAPTER IV.

LATER OPERATIONS ON THE LEHIGH.

THE first, or great southern field of anthracite coal in Pennsylvania, extends from near the Lehigh River, at Mauch Chunk, on the east, to Pottsville, and towards the river Susquehanna, in the neighborhood of Harrisburg, on the west, a distance of about sixty miles; in breadth it is pretty uniform, the maximum width not exceeding six or seven miles. The operations of the Lehigh Coal and Navigation Company in this region are confined to the eastern end of the basin, from Mauch Chunk westward to the Little Schuylkill River, at Tamaqua, a distance of about eleven miles, and most of the coal mined by the company is transported to the Lehigh River for shipment on the canal and railroads. Their land, according to the surveys and estimates of R. P. Rothwell, mining engineer, in 1869, comprises six thousand acres of coal land; the thickness of coal in the combined veins, forty-two feet, equal to four hundred and seventy-two millions of tons, or seventy-one thousand five hundred tons to the acre. The same authority says further: "That the Lehigh Coal and Navigation

Company possess one of the most magnificent coal properties in the world cannot be questioned, and that the quantity of coal is such as to allay all apprehensions for an abundant supply far into the future is indisputable."

It was in the centre of this region, about eight or nine miles from Mauch Chunk, at Summit Hill, at the point where Ginter discovered the coal, in the year 1791, and the previous companies had operated, where the first anthracite coal was ever mined for the market in this country, that White and Hazard commenced their operations. The coal cropped out near the surface, and the mining differed at first but little from ordinary stone quarrying; the earth and other covering of the coal was removed, and the operations carried on in the open air. G. F. Hauto describes the operation in a letter to a member of the legislature, Dec. 19, 1819, as follows:

"This mine, on our arrival, had quite an inconsiderable opening, like a moderate-sized stone-quarry; since which we have uncovered about two acres of coal land, removing all the earth, dirt, slate, etc. (about twelve feet deep), so as to leave a surface for the whole of that area of nothing but the purest coal, containing millions of bushels. We cut a passage through the rocks, so that now the teams drive right into the mine to load. The mine being situated near the summit of the moun-

COAL MINE AT SUMMIT HILL. Page 48.

tain, we are not troubled with water, and the coal quarries very easy. We have worked the stratum about thirty feet deep, and how much deeper it is we do not know."

The mine is thus described in an address published by the company in 1821: "The coal mine at present worked by the company lies on the top of a mountain, and appears to extend over some hundred acres of land, covered by about twelve feet of loose black dirt, resembling moist gunpowder, which can be removed by cattle with scrapers and thrown into the valley below, so as never to impede the work. The thickness of the coal is not known, but a shaft has been sunk in it thirty-five feet without penetrating through. More than an acre of mine has been uncovered by the company, and presents a huge rock of coal, which is easily quarried without blowing."

Nine years later, Professor Silliman, in his "Journal," thus describes the mines: "The coal is fairly laid open to view, and lies in stupendous masses, which are worked in open air exactly as in a stone-quarry. The excavation being in an angular area, and entered at different points by roads cut through the coal, in some places quite down to the lowest level, it has much the appearance of a vast fort, of which the central area is the parade-ground, and the upper escarpment is the platform for the cannon."

5*

From this point, the coal was in the commencement of the work hauled on the turnpike made by them for the purpose, which road is described by Hauto in the before-mentioned letter: "You know the ground between this, (Mauch Chunk,) and our principal coal mine, and that it would be hardly possible to find a more unfavorable one for the construction of a good road. The perpendicular elevation, from the river to this mine, is one thousand feet, the distance from the river upwards of eight miles. We constructed it in about three months, and most part of it in the winter season, a road having a regular declination of two and a half feet in every hundred. On it one horse can draw four tons with ease. . . . On this road we have now a sufficient number of teams to haul several thousand bushels per day." This turnpike road was superseded by the descending gravity railroad in 1827, and the coal carried by it to the river.

Mining coal from the open cut, exclusively, was continued up to about 1844, when the uncovering became so heavy, in consequence of the pitch of the veins, the company commenced mining in the Panther Creek Valley, and the old mining gradually diminished, until it has entirely ceased, it being now under ground in the usual manner.

This quarry was a point of much interest to the public in early days, affording an opportunity to view the coal in place, as nature had arranged it, such as could be seen nowhere else in the land; and where, also, the plan of mining could be appreciated.

The outlines of the first plan for a Lehigh Navigation and Coal Company were concluded in 1818. "The substance of which was a capital of two hundred thousand dollars divided into two hundred shares of stock; White, Hauto, and Hazard each retaining fifty shares, leaving fifty shares, or fifty thousand dollars, to be subscribed by others, who were to have all that was made up to eighteen per cent. on their capital, and we the residue. White, Hauto, and Hazard to assign to the company to be formed all their interest in the law,—obtained 20th March, 1818,—for the improvement of the navigation of the river, and the lease of twenty years of the Lehigh Coal Mine's lands; they to have the sole management, and conduct all the business, and be paid for their services."

There being two objects to be obtained, one, the improvement of the navigation of the river, the other, the mining and transporting of coal, there arose a diversity of opinion about the relative profits of the two interests, some having more confidence in the one and some in the other. This induced a division of their interests, and two companies were formed, one "The Lehigh Navigation Company," on the 10th of the 8th mo., 1818, for the improvement of the river; and on the 21st of the 10th mo. following, "The Lehigh Coal Company," for mining coal, and making a road from the mine to the river, and bringing it down the new navigation.

After these outlines of the company were agreed upon, they published a pamphlet, entitled "A Compendious View of the Law authorizing the Improvement of the River Lehigh," etc.; in which the following sanguine statements are made, as among the advantages to be obtained by the navigation of the river on the improved plan:

"The city of Philadelphia can be supplied with *coal* which is ascertained to be *twenty per cent. purer* than any of the same species which has come to this market from any other source, and at a *less price.*

"A market will be opened for an immense body of timber, which is now so completely locked up as not to be considered worth *stealing*, owing to the expense that would attend getting it to market.

"When the first grand section of the river is improved, (*which can be done in a few months,*) the land carriage to the Susquehanna at Berwick will be only thirty miles, over a turnpike *now made*, which will *immediately command the trade of that river, and turn it to Philadelphia.* When the second grand section is finished, the portage will be reduced to only *ten or twelve miles*, by a *railroad* contemplated to be made on excellent ground. By the Susquehanna and Lehigh the western counties of New York will be nearer, in point of expense, to Philadelphia than to Albany, and consequently a large portion of the produce, which now goes down the North River to New York, may be calculated on for the supply of Philadelphia.

"The New York grand canal when completed will bring the produce from the shores of Lake Erie. This produce can come, from the point where the canal crosses Seneca River to Philadelphia, in nearly *half the time, and consequently at half the expense*, that it can go by canal and North River to New York."

The tolls established by the act of the 20th of March, 1818, were "three cents per mile in the second grand section, and one cent per mile in the first, for every thousand feet of timber or lumber, or ton weight of other material passing down the river, *without any limit* as to the percentage to which they may amount."

Personal application and solicitation were made to a number of the leading capitalists of the day for subscription to the stock. Stephen Girard said "he formed no partnerships," and declined. Joseph Bonaparte respectfully declined joining in the enterprise, in a reply by letter through his secretary. One confessed, after being polite enough to listen to them, that he was "unable to appreciate their remarks"; another agreed to give them a hearing on the subject for "five minutes by the watch"; another appointed an evening for a hearing, and when called upon had gone to a party. One wrote "that his Wilkesbarre friends believed we could not be in earnest in our navigation." We replied, "if they would come and see us up to our waists in water, they would think it more earnest than fun." Notwithstanding considerable difficulty, they finally succeeded in obtaining subscriptions for the fifty thousand dollars stock, which was considered sufficient for the purpose.

They immediately proceeded to commence the work on the river. He says, 8 mo., 1818: "Bought a horse for one hundred dollars, a small dearborn wagon for sixty-five dollars, and rode up to Lausanne; but the wagon, being rather light, broke down twice before we arrived; this was, however, the only light carriage the company had until the summer of 1822, when it was so far worn out in the service that we sold it for five dollars. Began our work in the river with thirteen hands, at the mouth of Nesquehoning Creek, being the dividing point between the two grand sections. We rigged two scows about thirty-five feet long by fourteen feet wide for lodging- and eating-rooms for the men, about seventy in number. Also one scow for the managers' counting-house, storehouse and dwelling, and one for kitchen and bakehouse. These four boats were raised one story, of about six feet, and covered with board roofs. In these boats we placed all our stores, tools, and equipage. We had from two to four horses in the service, to bring wood, etc., for the kitchen, oven, etc. As it was our design to make the river navigable with small wing dams and channel walls, a single rift would not keep one hundred hands more than from one to six days to complete, so as we finished the work at one place we moved down with our floating town to the vicinity of the next. We continued living in our floating town until we were frozen up in the ice. The improvement being in a wilderness country, the workmen came from many nations and were strangers to us; we kept but little cash about us, paying the men in checks, according to agreement, which were not to be paid by the banks unless signed by two of us. Thus we offered no inducements for them to commit any violence on us in the wilderness country, for we were known to have no money on our persons. We were each clad in a complete suit of buckskin clothes, and were sometimes ourselves looked upon as suspicious persons in the country around."

He more fully describes their operations in a letter to a friend: "We improved the Lehigh River with wing dams in the first instance, as we could not raise the means, then, to make a slack-water navigation, and we did not know that the market would take from us enough anthracite coal, to justify the expense of a more perfect navigation. The distance we made with wing dams, etc., was forty-six miles, the fall about three hundred and sixty feet. Nearly all the rapids were covered with paving stones, so it cost us about twelve hundred dollars a mile exclusive of dams. Our design was to get eighteen inches depth of water by twenty-five feet width; so that by contracting the channel at the rifts to this width with the paving stones, and raising the wings and channel walls no more than to hold the eighteen or twenty inches of water, they stood well enough. The channel walls, or walls parallel to the channel, were about six times the width of their height; the walls across the stream, eight or ten times their height. The channels as straight as possible, they kept themselves clean."

In their first report to the stockholders, dated Dec. 31, 1818, they say: "The managers commenced their operations on the Lehigh, on the 19th of August, and concluded them on the 19th of November. During that time, they estimate that they have made, in the river, dams amounting in length to about thirteen thousand feet, and supposed to contain upwards of sixteen thousand perches of stone. By these dams the parts of the lower section that were considered the worst have been made navigable at all seasons of *common* low water, and a *fresh* dam of four hundred and fifty feet long is nearly finished, which they trust will accommodate the public with a navigation to Easton the ensuing season."

But the following year they early discovered that they had not sufficient water for their purposes. Josiah White writes: "We found the natural flow of the water in the Lehigh was insufficient to give us eighteen inches depth and twenty feet width, as required by law; the water subsiding much below the mark we had made, on the best information we were able to procure from those on the river, who professed to know all about it; and were obliged to make a great experiment to obtain the water, by artificial freshets; and if we failed in this, our whole work would be exploded and have to be abandoned.

"I devoted myself for several weeks to form a plan of sluice that would answer, and be cheaply made, and safe at all stages of the water. I succeeded in producing the lock and sluice called the '*Bear-trap*,' a name the workmen gave it, while we were experimenting with it on Mauch Chunk Creek, to elude the curiosity of persons who teased them with inquiries as to what we were making. We put up about twelve of these locks and dams in 1819, and proved them, so as to determine that they would answer our purpose, and I took out a patent for them in the 12th mo., 1819.*

"As our work was generally in the water seven or eight months in the year, and my portion of it being to lay out the walls and channels in the river, pile stone as marks, etc., I dressed in clothes suitable: a red flannel shirt, roundabout coat, cap, strong shoes with a hole cut in their toe to let out the water; our clothing being made of coarse cloth, and buckskin tanned in oil, to turn the water. In the summer, during the day, I was as much in the water as out of it, for three seasons; allowing the clothing to dry on my back; when wet, I kept up the circulation by walking about my business, and seldom caught cold; sleeping at night in one of our boats, in a bunk, with blankets, the first two years, without a bed, in the same manner as the workmen.

"Our improvements on the river were this year (1819) extended to the Lehigh Water Gap, at the Blue Mountain, ten miles below Mauch Chunk. We fully proved by the artificial navigation our ability to send such a regular supply of coal to market as would supply all the demand. The present arrangement we considered sufficient to test the question, whether the use of coal by the

---

* See Appendix No. 1 for a plan and description of this lock.

public would so increase, as to justify a better, or whether we should by limited sales be confined to the present descending navigation. If a large demand should arise, it would justify a change."

They had, however, expended the whole of the capital of the company this year, and the works were not so well secured against the winter freshets and ice as would have been desirable. He says:

"It was the first instance in Pennsylvania of employing so large a number of workmen in the wilderness; it was impossible to tell how we should succeed in getting them until we made the trial, and not putting up enough of our work to prove its feasibility would have been fatal to our getting any more capital to finish it. To do this, we had to spread the work over a sufficient line for experiment, and risk and trust to being able, in the early part of the winter, to perfectly inclose or cover the work against the freshets. Notwithstanding we had spent all our capital, we kept as many men employed through the winter of 1819–20 as we could well get along with, and I supplied the necessary funds until we got another subscription, and the public knew nothing of our pecuniary difficulties; as it would have been ruinous to have broken up and disbanded our men, and would have confirmed the public in what they had predicted, another failure."

It being found that the interests of the Navigation Company and the Coal Company were not identical, and gave rise to some clashing, it was concluded to amalgamate them in the spring of 1820, "on the express condition that twenty thousand dollars of the stock should be taken, and the new stock called 'the Lehigh Navigation and Coal Company.'" This small addition of capital was with difficulty obtained, and not until twelve thousand dollars of it were taken by White & Hazard; more than six thousand of which Josiah White had advanced, to carry the concern through the winter.

"In the year 1820, the dams and locks being repaired, the first anthracite coal was sent to market by our *artificial navigation;* the whole quantity sent was three hundred and sixty-five tons; this proved more than enough for family supplies in Philadelphia, and the company was indebted to the rolling-mills, etc., for taking off this stock, although they never asked more than eight dollars and forty cents a ton; whereas, the company previous to ours asked as much as they could get, and obtained twenty-one dollars a ton for it. This seemed to confirm the doubtful, who in the beginning admitted we had plenty of coal, but that the prejudice of the community would be against its use in the family."

The difficulty experienced in burning it as a domestic fuel, and for cooking purposes,—which for want of experience and proper appliances was a very great drawback to its introduction and use,—he endeavored to obviate, and made many experiments for that purpose, with different kinds of grates and fixtures; and in his office, at his house in Philadelphia, had a fire in operation for the inspection of the public, which showed its complete practicability for these purposes.

They again expended all their capital this year, and the following spring endeavored to obtain more funds by subscription.

His account continues: "The difficulties of selling more stock seemed to increase; our capital had been increased to one hundred and twenty-five thousand dollars, and the citizens of Philadelphia did not incline to introduce coal into their families, and many of the stockholders said their money had all been thrown away, for, if we finally made the river navigable and the works safe, which they much doubted, the community would not have our coal, and it was not believed that the other articles of trade on the navigation would be enough to make it pay. A new difficulty also presented at a place called 'The Slates,' where a ridge ran across the river, where it was four hundred feet or more in breadth, with generally a level top, except being full of small breaks, through the ledges over which we had carried the channel; but it was found the wing walls being so long through the slate ridges, they would not hold water in the channels, so that the cheapest improvement to obviate this, in the opinion of the managers, would be a large dam, which they estimated could not be completed for less than twenty thousand dollars. The difficulties in obtaining a further subscription were so great, that they could not be overcome before the spring of 1821, and then fifty thousand dollars were subscribed under the following extraordinary circumstances: all the old subscribers agreed that the subscriptions to the fifty thousand dollars, called new stock, should in future draw all the income until they obtained three per cent. semi-annual dividends, and then the balance of the profit went to the old subscribers, until they also had received the same; and the stock was to continue in this way until there was profit enough to pay all three per cent. semi-annual dividends, and then the stock to be equal, etc. And, in addition, that White & Hazard give a bonus of their reversionary stock of ten thousand dollars to new subscribers. Upon obtaining the subscription the 'slate dam' was immediately commenced, and with some difficulties completed in this year."

The earliest records of the company having been accidentally destroyed, the first election of officers on record occurred on the 23d of the 5th month, 1821, when the following persons were selected: President, John Cox; Treasurer, Jonathan Fell; Secretary, Jacob Shoemaker; Acting Managers, Josiah White and Erskine Hazard, who appear to have constituted the whole board of management.*

"It was believed at the close of the year 1821, that it would be best to endeavor to procure an act of incorporation; for, although we shipped and sent to Philadelphia one thousand and seventy-three tons of coal, still, the consumption by families in Philadelphia was insufficient to take this small quantity, the balance being sold to factories. The work, also, was still considered an experiment, as to making and rendering the navigation permanent. Therefore the managers were of the unanimous opinion that more money could not be raised, as all our property was pledged at the last subscription, and that we had no security to offer, unless we obtained a charter of incorporation, so as to risk nothing more than the stock any individual might subscribe." The charter was obtained on the 13th of February, 1822, entitled "An act to incorporate the Lehigh Coal and Navigation Company." The capital stock was to consist of one million of dollars, to be divided into shares of fifty dollars each,

---

* The only survivor of the early managers of the Lehigh Coal and Navigation Company is our venerable townsman, John McAllister, elected in 1831, and ten years in office; still green in old age, and enjoying the respect and esteem of those who have the privilege of his acquaintance.

of which the old stock was to constitute a part. No part of this act was to impair or repeal any of the provisions of the former act, entitled "An act to improve the navigation of the river Lehigh," passed the 20th of March, 1818, except so much as was altered or supplied by this.

In the years 1822 and 1823 the descending navigation was perfected, and the company contributed four or five thousand dollars to improve the channels in the Delaware River. The works were inspected by commissioners and reported finished, and the governor issued his license, on the "17th of January, 1823, authorizing them to take toll;" it having been in use for a year or two previously, but no toll taken then nor afterwards until 1827.

"Inasmuch as by the descending navigation we obtained but one trip from our boats, (as they were taken to pieces and the lumber sold in Philadelphia,) it was found impossible to continue the coal business, even in its then small way, without clearing out and contracting the channels for about sixteen miles above Mauch Chunk, to the pine forests, to procure a sufficient supply of lumber for that purpose. This, however, was no small matter; in this distance there was a fall in the river exceeding three hundred feet, and the transportation over rapids; the bottom was rocky and particularly hard and difficult, and so forbidding were the shores that, except along the channel of the river, it was impossible to transport any supplies for the use of the workmen; so the provisions, etc., had to be conveyed to the upper end, to the mouth of Laurel Run, (eighteen miles,) and floated down the river. No raft had, as far as known, before these channels were made, ever passed from above down to Nesquehoning Creek, and from thence down the river was only navigable for rafts in times of high freshets.

"Before these channels were made, we attempted to procure planks from above by floating them down the rapids, but this was a failure, as they were worn out or broken against the rocks before their arrival; and in floating logs, many of them were carried off in the freshets, and were lost or stolen.

"About this time we contrived the present plan of weighing coal with a scale, with the dish resting on four knife-edged fulcrums and compound levers; we weighed the wagons with it. This plan of scale has now obtained general use, from those of small size up to those large enough to weigh loaded boats. In the year 1823 five thousand eight hundred tons of coal were sent down the Lehigh, and about one thousand tons of it was left on hand unsold in the following spring. There still continued a disinclination to use it much in families, and persons passing our coal wharf constantly told us we had overstocked the market. The next year, (1824,) however, with many misgivings, there was sent down the *enormous quantity*, as it was thought, of nine thousand five hundred and forty-one tons, and predictions were made that not the half of it would be sold. But this did not prove to be the case, for the public, seeing that the supply was likely to be permanently adequate, and it suitable for family use, and the price steady at eight dollars and forty cents per ton, began more generally to inquire after and use it. Manufacturers of stoves and grates, in the winter of 1824–25, first began to notify the public of desirable and preferable patterns for burning it. Several patriotic ladies exhibited their sample fires; among them the widow Guest, in Sansom Street, stood the most conspicuous; and of grate-makers, Jacob F. Walter took quite a leading part. This winter may be considered quite *the turning-point* in the use of anthracite coal."

In the year 1825 the company sent to market twenty-eight thousand three hundred and ninety-three tons of coal. This year the Schuylkill Navigation Company began the coal business on the canal by sending forward seven thousand one hundred and forty-three tons.

"In the year 1826 the desirable event of equalizing the stock took place, and the company sent to market thirty-one thousand two hundred and eighty tons of coal."

In the year 1827 the railroad from Mauch Chunk to the mines was made. This was placed mainly on the route of the old wagon road from the mines to the river, originally laid out, in 1818, by Josiah White and Erskine Hazard personally, the grades then being 4½ miles, 2 feet descent; ¾ mile, 1.6 foot; ¾ mile, 1 foot; 2½ miles, 2½ feet descent in 100 feet. The elevation of the old coal mine above the Lehigh River at Mauch Chunk, at the point where the coal was delivered into boats, is nine hundred and thirty-six feet; the distance to the river from the mines is about nine miles, the road constantly descending by an irregular declivity. At the bank of the river an inclined plane is constructed about seven hundred yards long, with a declivity of two hundred and fifty feet at the bottom, down a chute, into the boats on the water. The whole was completed, so as to pass coal over it regularly, in about four months, and is the *first railroad* in this country ever constructed for the transportation *of coal*, and, with one or two trifling exceptions, for any other purpose. The sleepers were laid four feet apart, upon a foundation of stone; the rail itself was of rolled iron bars, about three-eighths of an inch thick and one and a half inches in width, upon a wooden foundation. The loaded wagons each carried one and a half tons of coal, and descended in gangs of six, eight, or ten connected together, each gang attended by two men to regulate the velocity of the descent. The wagons weighed about one thousand two hundred pounds each. The empty wagons were returned to the mines by horses or mules, each animal taking three or four of them back in three hours. They descended to the river with the coal in cars constructed for their use. The time occupied in the descent was about thirty minutes. The cost of this road was thirty-eight thousand seven hundred and twenty-six dollars, or three thousand and fifty dollars per mile; the length, including lateral and branch roads, to and into the mines, was about twelve and a half miles.

The managers say in their report: "One hundred and forty-six railroad wagons have been made, and the utility of the road proved by transporting twenty-seven thousand seven hundred and seventy tons of coal, at a saving over the turnpike of sixty-four and three-quarters cents per ton; and has produced a saving this year of over fifteen thousand dollars, and, in mining the coal and boating department, of sixteen cents per ton, thus reducing the cost of the coal more than eighty cents per ton: the whole amount this year sent to market being thirty-two thousand and seventy-four tons. There were also constructed nearly fifteen miles of boats for its transportation, taking from the stump seven million four hundred and twelve thousand one hundred and eighty-three feet of lumber."

Before taking leave of the old descending navigation of the river Lehigh, it may be well to describe it more fully in Josiah White's own words: "As the artificial navigation is now abandoned, and a canal and slack-water introduced, it is due to give its character. The river had twelve small dams and 'bear-trap' locks of from three to six feet in height, from Mauch Chunk to Lehigh Water Gap, (eleven miles,) and nine miles below, at 'The Slates,' a large dam and 'bear-trap' lock, one hundred and thirty feet long and thirty feet wide, made for a lift-lock; and, seventeen miles below 'The Slates,' another dam six or seven feet high, with an ascending lock like that at 'The Slates.' A man was stationed on the front coal ark and rode down to the second lock, when he got off and let down the gates, (taking from thirty seconds to a minute for the purpose,) and then resumed his station on the ark again, by which time there would be sufficient water passing through the lock, and the water above beginning to fall; they then passed through to the next lock with the current of water, when the same lock tender repeated the operation as before, through the twelve locks, to the Gap, leaving the aperture open until the dam emptied itself, and then walked back in the afternoon, putting up all the lock-gates, so as to hold the water for the freshet of next day; the accumulated water in the first pond being sufficient to fill the channel to the head of the next dam, and so on to the Gap; and the accumulation of water in the twelve dams, then, (at the Gap,) carried the fleet of arks of from six to nine boats, or nest of arks, down nine miles to 'The Slates'; the pond being here one mile long, which, together with the water from above, carried the arks down the river to the thirty-seven mile dam, seventeen miles below 'The Slates,' and thence down to the Delaware, and gave four inches of a freshet in that river. We have sent as many sections at once as would make from one hundred and ninety to two hundred feet in length; the average size of boats being one hundred and forty to one hundred and fifty feet in length, sixteen feet wide, and drawing fourteen to sixteen inches of water; the sections being sixteen to twenty-five feet long, the whole being in charge of a front and hind oarsman and three hands; carrying seventy to one hundred and twenty tons. During the three last years that we used these boats, we made an average of ten or twelve consecutive miles of them yearly, entirely from the tree; one set of workmen making a single section in three-quarters of an hour, and seven or eight boats of from five to seven sections in a day; the plank being planed and jointed by water-power at Laurel Run, and by crank- and man-power at Mauch Chunk. The caulking was done with half-inch, square white pine strips, put corner-ways to fit into grooves made for the purpose in the plank, and finished with rushes brought from below Philadelphia, and rough tow. For the three years above mentioned, we carried forty thousand tons of coal a year; and the boats were knocked to pieces in Philadelphia and the iron sent back to Mauch Chunk; the boatmen mostly walking back at first, but in the later years they hired teams to take them."

CHAPTER V.

THE ASCENDING NAVIGATION ON THE LEHIGH.

THE value of coal as a fuel was at length beginning to be fully appreciated by the public. From a report to the Legislature of Pennsylvania by the Committee on Internal Improvements, in the spring of 1829, the following is extracted:

"It may truly be observed that each successive year develops new views in relation to the rich treasure Pennsylvania has in coal. A recent memorial from the Lyceum of Natural History in New York states the amount paid within one year for fuel, for domestic purposes and steamboats, in the city of New York, at two million four hundred thousand dollars. Governor Clinton, in his last official message, remarks, that New York is compelled to resort to the coal of Pennsylvania; and he says, the quantity which will be wanted for that State is estimated at two millions of tons. It has now become obvious that coal will constitute the chief article of fuel, not only in the city and State of New York, but in many parts of all the States on the seaboard. Coal has become an object of vast national importance, and it will soon be a part of the public policy of many States of the Union to facilitate the means of procuring it from the State of Pennsylvania. Our State may proudly say, that the bounty of nature has made her mountains the grand repository of this precious mineral, and also of iron; and every ton which is extracted from the mines will be tributary to her wealth and greatness." In conclusion, the Committee say: "The genius of William Penn recognized the policy of navigable communications in Pennsylvania more than half a century before a canal was constructed in his native coûntry; and our predecessors, the inhabitants of the land he planted, were the first among the members of the American family who ran a level or measured waters with a view to canal navigation."

The managers of the company being assured of the certain success of their undertaking, both as regarded the improvement of the river and the introduction of coal into general use, immediately saw the necessity of changing the plan of their navigation, and also the manner of constructing boats. Previously to this the company had purchased nearly all the stock of the old coal mine company, thereby becoming the owners of the coal lands. Josiah White says: "In the spring of 1827 it was finally concluded to begin and prosecute the ascending navigation; for that undertaking the company employed Canvass White as the principal engineer, he having established a practical character for that profession equal to any in the country. The next difficult point to decide was the size of the navigation; whether it should be for boats carrying a burden of twenty-five tons, or for a greater burden. Most of the engineers who had written on the subject in England and America recommended the twenty-five ton navigation. The acting managers (White & Hazard) contended for a navigation sufficient for boats of one hundred and thirty to one hundred and fifty tons burden; they argued that as the Lehigh and Delaware afforded plenty of water for the largest class of boats, it would be suicidal policy to permanently deprive the company and the public of the very best application of all the means nature had afforded, particularly so as our company had coal enough to supply the United States,—and, in our case, as coal would be by far the greatest article carried on the canal,—so that no boat need ever descend to Philadelphia with less than a full load; and that a large boat would require but the same crew as a small one, consequently every ton transported could be carried cheaper by this arrangement. After considerable debate, it was finally decided to make the locks conform to the size of the Chesapeake and Delaware Canal: twenty-two feet wide, one hundred feet long, and five feet depth of water, and the width of the canal at the bottom forty-five feet."

This important decision was a great advantage at the time, and has since then saved the company from the necessity of enlarging their locks, to meet the demands of the trade and competition with railroads, which most of the other canals have been obliged to do.

The engineer corps, under Canvass White, as furnished by Solomon W. Roberts, one of the party, and nephew of Josiah White, were: on the upper division, commencing one mile below Mauch Chunk, Isaac A. Chapman, of Wilkesbarre, and W. Milner Roberts and Solomon W. Roberts, of Philadelphia; on the middle division were Anthony B. Warford, of New York, Benj. Aycrigg, of New Jersey, and Ashbel Welch; on the lower division were John Hopkins and Geo. E. Hoffman, both of New York, and Wm. K. Huffnagle, of Philadelphia. Edward Miller, of Philadelphia, soon after joined the corps, afterwards chief engineer of the Catawissa, the Sunbury and Erie, Pacific Railroads, Morris Canal, etc. From an obituary notice of Edward Miller, by Solomon W. Roberts, is quoted the following: "Mr. White had been one of the principal engineers on the Erie Canal of New York, and he was a gentleman of fine character and of much experience. He had made pedestrian tours along the lines of the principal canals of Great Britain, and he was a man of sterling integrity and of great industry. The resident engineer was Sylvester Welch, a man of remarkable energy of character, who planned the Portage Railroad, and directed its construction across the Alleghany Mountain, and who was afterwards the chief engineer of the State of Kentucky. With him was his brother, Ashbel Welch, since the chief engineer of various important works in New Jersey, and for several years, until the recent leasing of the lines, the president of the united companies of that State. On the Lehigh at the same time were W. Milner Roberts, now the chief engineer of the Northern Pacific Railroad, Solomon W. Roberts, now chief engineer and superintendent of the North Pennsylvania Railroad, A. B. Warford, Geo. E. Hoffman, Benjamin Aycrigg, and several other well-known engineers. It was a good school."

Instructions were given by the company to the engineer "to examine the ground from Mauch Chunk to Easton, along the valley of the Lehigh, and to report to the board the plan of a canal and river improvement, and an estimate of the cost of the work. Canals to be made in lieu of river improvements only, when they would be cheaper." And after giving the dimensions of the canal and locks, etc., as before stated: "If the foregoing stipulation were not such as, in his estimation, best adapted to the situation and expressed business of the company, to propose such a plan, with an estimate of the cost of it, as he would of his own unbiased judgment recommend." His report was in conformity with the view of the company, that "the length of canal would be thirty-five and three-fourths miles, and ten miles of pools, with tow-paths the whole distance, and the estimate of the expense seven hundred and eighty-one thousand three hundred and three dollars."

This improved navigation was commenced in 1827, and vigorously prosecuted, and completed in about two years; commissioners were appointed by the governor of the State, 6 mo. 26, 1829, who reported on the third of the following month, that the work was completed according to law as far as Mauch Chunk; they say: "We were indeed surprised to find a *new* canal forty-five feet wide at the bottom, sixty feet at the top, calculated for five feet depth of water, stand as well as this has done. Wherever there is any danger to be apprehended to the bank, from the rise of water in the river, the bank of the canal is protected by good slope walls. The locks are composed of good stone, laid in hydraulic cement; the insides are cased with plank and the space between the covering and the wall grouted with the same kind of cement. Notwithstanding the size of the locks, everything being new and the gatekeepers inexperienced, the average time of passing the locks was about five minutes. There are forty-five lift-locks in number, of six, seven, eight and nine feet fall, all of twenty-two feet by one hundred feet, except the four upper ones, near Mauch Chunk, which are thirty feet by one hundred and thirty feet, overcoming a fall of three hundred and sixty and eighty-seven-one-hundredth feet, in a distance of forty-six and three-fourths miles, and there are also six guard-locks. The dams are eight in number; they are built of timber and stone in a very substantial manner, with stone abutments, and of the following heights: five, thirteen, eight, sixteen, twelve, six, seven and one-half, and ten feet from surface to surface. On the whole, the works appear to have been constructed with a view to service and durability, and the corporation, in our opinion, is entitled to much commendation for the promptness and energy displayed in the prosecution and completion of this great public improvement."

The following is quoted from the managers' report for 1830: "They wish not improperly to vaunt the merits of the work thus spoken of, but they believe they may with perfect truth state that there is no work of the kind in the country, of equal length, that can compare with it in point of magnitude, permanency, and efficiency. In the words of the acting manager (J. White), 'there has been no money expended for ornament, though no money has been spared to render the work sound and permanent.' "

They state "that the length of our line of improvement is forty-six and three-quarters miles: thirty-six and three-quarters miles of canal, and ten miles of pools, with a towing-path throughout the line; and that the company has expended on the river since the commencement, including the amount paid White Hazard & Hauto, for their property rights and privileges, about one million five hundred and fifty-eight thousand dollars."

"The managers feel bound, while speaking of their works and business on the Lehigh, to comment for a moment on the long-continued and faithful services of their acting manager, Josiah White, to whose active and energetic conduct, in all things connected with the interests of the company, they owe much for his direction, aid, and advice promptly afforded in all emergencies.

"The company mined twenty-seven thousand one hundred and fifty tons of coal this year, and shipped from Mauch Chunk twenty-five thousand one hundred and ten tons."

The managers, in their report for 1831, say that the Morris Canal was ready for use a few weeks of the latter part of the year, and "a considerable number of boats, laden chiefly with coal from Mauch Chunk, were passed through the whole line from the Delaware to Newark Bay. It is a highly gratifying circumstance that this canal is now completed, and its successful operation during the short period referred to furnishes an assurance that in the coming season it will enable us greatly to extend our business with the New York market, and with the extensive agricultural and manufacturing districts through which the canal passes."

The State of Pennsylvania began the Delaware Canal in 1828, and in 1830 the Canal Commissioners, in their report, remark: "The filling of the canal for navigation, in its whole course, commenced in October, 1830," and that "twenty-five miles are navigable;" but they add that "a part of the work first constructed has proved defective, and requires extensive repairs. This last observation has been verified by the fact that since that time the two supervisors have expended ninety-seven thousand three hundred and thirty-nine dollars and fifty-one cents on repairs, and introducing feeders, and the whole line is not yet ready for navigation. The original plan and construction of large portions of this division have proved to be exceedingly defective, and although every exertion has been made throughout the year, by the officers on the line, to fill the whole canal with water, yet their efforts have heretofore proved unsuccessful. The porous nature of the soil along the Delaware has demonstrated the fallacy of the original design of feeding the entire sixty miles of canal from the Lehigh."

The imperfect navigation of the Delaware Canal

was a serious drawback to the trade of the Lehigh Canal, and after some solicitation Josiah White was induced to undertake the task of endeavoring to remedy its defects, and for that purpose he first received the appointment of engineer of this work, and afterwards that of canal commissioner in the year 1831.

He says: "It has been frequently said of late years that the Delaware Canal was made for the accommodation of the Lehigh coal trade, and that consequently we were under great obligation to the State for making it, etc.; and that they made the locks eleven feet wide for our accommodation, whereas we wished them twenty-two feet, the same dimensions as our own; but as they would not make them to please us, we advised that they should be half that width, that, as two boats passed our locks at a time, one boat might fit their locks, and pass one at a time. But our view was *not* to canal along the Delaware, but to make a *channel and slack-water* navigation, which is shown in a draft and petition which we sent to Harrisburg in the years 1823 and 1824, and used all our influence to get a law to make a navigation in accordance therewith.*

"With this arrangement it might require from

---

* See Appendix No. 2 for plan and description of the proposed navigation for the Delaware River.

six to twelve locks in the Delaware, and the remainder of the navigation mere channels. We expected to obtain four feet of water at the lowest time, and five feet at other times, and that it would carry steamboats of one hundred and fifty tons burden, and for which we had made four locks in advance on the Lehigh, thirty feet wide and one hundred and thirty feet long, so as to have a steamboat navigation of the same capacity to Mauch Chunk. Had we succeeded in this in 1824, there can be but little doubt the Lehigh would have sent three-fourths of all the anthracite coal reaching tide water for many years to come, and we should have drawn the coal trade from Tuscarora, and perhaps from Pottsville, as Pottsville, via Mauch Chunk, to New York, is two hundred and two miles, and by the Schuylkill Canal it is two hundred and thirty-two miles; the Schuylkill Canal being but twenty-five tons capacity, and ours one hundred and fifty tons. We should also have had all the coal trade from the second coal region, as well as that also from Wilkesbarre and Wyoming.

"The law for improving the Delaware by canal was brought about by Colonel Eyre, of Easton, then a State senator, for the purpose, we then believed, of opposing our plan of a slack-water navigation.

"The State began the work in the autumn of 1828, and we began the Lehigh Canal in the spring of the same year. Ours was finished and in use the fall of 1829, but the Delaware Canal not until three years after. The contractors were allowed to fill up the canal to bottom with bad material, and when reported finished it would not hold water."

The many defects in the Delaware Canal, and the short supply of water, were causes of great disappointment and vexation in the use of the navigation. At one time the whole volume of the Lehigh River, at Easton, was fed into this canal; but the water failed to reach New Hope, having all leaked out on the way. By thoroughly repairing; the use of better material; by harrowing and rolling the bottom; and by a dam and water-wheels on the Delaware River at Well's Falls; and a number of additional feeders, by which a large amount of water was thrown into the canal, they at length succeeded in making it navigable under the management of Josiah White.

The report of the Lehigh Coal and Navigation Company, for the year 1832, on this subject states: "In our last report we anticipated the full use of that canal during the past season, but the occurrence of a very unusual ice freshet in the spring frustrated our hopes, by destroying a considerable portion of the exposed parts of the upper section of the canal, which was proved to have been constructed in a very unskillful manner. The repair of this damage occupied much time, and, when effected, the water had become too low to saturate the porous soil over which the canal passed, and fill it a sufficient depth for navigation. Several feeders were constructed to supply the deficiency, and it was not until the 23d of July last that the first boats arrived at Bristol, each loaded with twenty tons of coal.

"The loading was gradually increased twenty-five, thirty, thirty-five, forty, forty-five, and finally to fifty tons.

"The company is only now placed where it ought to have been in July, 1829, when the Lehigh Canal was finished, it having been commenced in the same season as the State Canal on the Delaware, which has not half as much lockage, and but half the capacity of the Lehigh Canal." In their report for 1834, it is said, "there has been no material interruption of the navigation on the Delaware Division of the Pennsylvania Canal." The total quantity of coal shipped from Mauch Chunk during the year 1834 was one hundred and six thousand five hundred tons, the greater portion of which passed into the Delaware Division of the State Canal.

Upon the completion of the Delaware Canal, the operations of the Lehigh Company were much simplified, as it did not, as heretofore, require a large number of men to obtain the lumber, and to build the boats necessary to carry the coal to market,—boats which never returned, and had to be replaced by new ones.

In 1833 the railroad connecting the mines at Room Run with the Lehigh Canal was completed. These mines are situated on the northern side of the coal basin, at a break in the mountain caused by the passage of the Room Run Creek, which affords an outlet into the valley of the Nesquehoning about five miles from the Lehigh River. Along the side of the mountain a very substantial railroad was constructed. The rails were firmly set in cast-iron knees, bolted to stone blocks, upon which the coal was brought down to the head of an inclined plane, at the bottom of which it was shipped into boats. This was also a gravity road with reciprocating planes; and an important feeder to the trade on the canal.

The Beaver Meadow Railroad, commencing in the second coal-field, at the town of the same name, nineteen miles from Mauch Chunk, was chartered in 1830, and finished in 1836. It extended to Parryville (twenty-five miles), and shipped the coal there on the Lehigh Canal, six miles below Mauch Chunk.

The Hazelton Railroad was commenced in 1836 in the second coal region, and connected with the Beaver Meadow Railroad, at Weatherly, in 1838.

CHAPTER VI.

MAUCH CHUNK AND THE UPPER SECTION OF THE LEHIGH RIVER.

THE picturesque town of Mauch Chunk (Bear Mountain) had its origin at the same time that White, Hazard, and Hauto commenced the coal mining and the navigation of the river. The site was selected from the emergency of the circumstances. The original intention appears to have been to place the town at Lausanne, a mile above; but the owners of the land there declined selling their property, under the vain hope that there was coal underlying it, to be obtained in due time. The geological formations of the country not being understood, it was not then known that it was beyond the coal measures. Necessity therefore obliged them to locate the town in the romantic gorge of Mauch Chunk Creek, and on the borders of the Lehigh River; since which it has steadily advanced up the valley of the creek, and the sides and top of the adjacent mountains, until it has attained its present dimensions. It is a peculiar and attractive-looking place, and from the first has had an industrious and enterprising population.

G. F. A. Hauto gives this description of Mauch Chunk about one year after its birth: "We have erected about forty buildings for different purposes, among which is a saw-mill driven by the river for the purpose of sawing stuff for the use of the navigation. It has a gang to which twenty-four saws belong, cutting about twenty thousand feet per day, on one side; and a circular saw on the other. One other saw-mill driven by the Mauch Chunk (Creek); a grist-mill, a mill for the saving of labor for the construction of wagons, etc., is also driven by the creek,—smitheries, with eight fires, workshops, dwellings, wharves, etc. We have cut about fifteen thousand saw logs, and cleared four hundred acres of land."

In the year 1821, Elizabeth White and her four children joined her husband in this mountain home. She was ready and willing, since the death of her fond mother, which had occurred in the seventy-second year of her age, to go at the call of duty from the comforts of a city life to this new residence in the wilderness, to be with her husband, and thus obviate the necessity of their often protracted separation from each other, during the building of the improvements on the river and the development of the coal trade. The next year a comfortable house was provided for them upon the hill-side, above the beautiful river, with spacious grounds, adorned with rocks and forest-trees; later, an extensive inclosure, styled "The Park," contained elk, deer, etc., for the amusement of the children, whose gratification and instruction were always a source of pleasure to their parents, who spared no reasonable expense for their rational enjoyment.

Here, in 1826, his aged mother closed her life in the family of her son, in the eighty-second year of her age. Their residence at Mauch Chunk covered a period of about nine years; and as the character and novelty of this unique place, with the curious works and appliances, in connection with the operations of the company, attracted the attention of the public, their house became the frequent resort of visitors, who shared the open and free hospitality extended to strangers by the family, whilst enjoying the mountain scenery and examining the operations in the vicinity.

In 1831, the works of the company being so far completed as not to require his constant attention, the family returned to Philadelphia, where they settled at the corner of Seventh and Arch Streets; and soon after a heavy domestic affliction was experienced by the parents, in the loss of their only remaining son, the following winter, a very promising young man, in the nineteenth year of his age. This sad bereavement was the greatest sorrow they had yet known, and cast a blight on the future. Previously two sons had died in childhood.

Perhaps in this relation it may be well to anticipate, and state, that in the year 1846 the family removed to the dwelling No. 526 Arch Street, which proved to be the last earthly home of Josiah White and his wife, who survived him over four years. She deceased in the spring of 1855, being in the seventy-fifth year of her age.

At the annual meeting of the stockholders, held 1st mo. 9, 1832, information being communicated to the meeting that Josiah White had resigned his office as acting manager at Mauch Chunk, and removed his residence to Philadelphia, it was "Resolved, that the thanks of the stockholders be presented to him for his able and valuable services during the long period of his arduous appointment." In his report, made at the same time, he states: "It is now the twenty-second year since I commenced operations in the work of internal improvement at the Falls of Schuylkill, in which time I have been absent from that kind of service but very few days. It is also the fourteenth year since I began with my colleague, Erskine Hazard, our labors at Mauch Chunk and on the Lehigh. The whole work is now done. The line of navigation may be considered as complete from Mauch Chunk to Philadelphia by the Delaware Canal, and to New York by the Morris Canal." The Morris Canal had just been finished, and put in operation in 1831.

He continued to feel a deep interest in the welfare of the company, being a prominent manager, and frequently visiting the different points of interest where the extension or improvement of the works was going on, with or without the other managers; and also maintained an active correspondence with the engineer, superintendent, and other officers until near the close of his life. He found many objects, also, to engage his attention as a citizen; liberally giving aid and encouragement to many of the benevolent, educational, and moral institutions of his day; being much interested in the welfare, prosperity, and growth of the country in its manufactures, mechanic arts, general industry, and, particularly, in the extension of internal improvements by railroads and canals.

In the year 1835 the company commenced the construction of the navigation on the upper grand section of the canal from Mauch Chunk to White Haven. The immense fall in the river rendered the use of ordinary locks out of the question. They, therefore, conceived the design of making a navigation on a grander and bolder scale than ever yet attempted in the history of such enterprises, both as regards the height of the dams and the capacity of the locks. The whole distance from Mauch Chunk to the head of the river at White Haven is about twenty-six miles; the lockage in that distance six hundred feet; the number of dams were twenty, of locks twenty-nine; the height of the dams from sixteen to fifty-eight feet; the size of the locks twenty by one hundred feet, and the lifts from ten to thirty feet. By the peculiar construction of the wicket-gates in these, they could be filled and emptied in the time usual for ordinary locks; by these means both expense and time were saved over the common mode; the locks not being more than one-fourth the number that would have been required of the other kind, and the time consumed in the voyage lessened in the same ratio. The principal part of this navigation was slack-water, there being twenty and a half miles of pools and five and a half miles of canal; the canal being sixty feet wide at top water, forty feet at bottom, and of the depth of five feet. The dams were made of crib-work, filled in with stone, in the ordinary manner, as dams are constructed on the Lehigh; and the locks with stone walls, cemented and grouted together. The locks were of sufficient capacity to pass two boats at a time.

The work was completed in the 6th mo., 1838; the descending navigation from Stoddartsville, with bear-trap locks, to connect with the ascending navigation at White Haven, a distance of twelve miles, was finished the previous year; thus making a continuous navigation, from the head-waters of the Lehigh at Stoddartsville, with Easton on the Delaware, and from thence, by the Delaware

Canal, to tide-water at Bristol, on the Delaware, a distance of one hundred and forty-four miles.

The plan for the navigation of the upper Lehigh was designed by Josiah White and Erskine Hazard, and was under the care and management of Edwin A. Douglas, civil engineer of the company, a man of ingenuity, competency, and untiring energy of purpose, whom few difficulties could appall or deter from the execution of his duties. He continued to be the company's engineer and superintendent until his death, in 1860.

The following is taken from the report of the commissioners, appointed in 1838 by Governor Ritner, to examine and report the condition of the work on the upper section of the navigation: "The dimensions of the largest of the locks (No. 27, called the 'Pennsylvania Lock') being as follows: twenty-seven feet thickness of solid wall at the bottom and ten feet on the top; thirty feet lift, three feet working guard, chamber twenty feet in width and one hundred feet in length, eighty-six feet clear of the swing of the gates, and containing nine thousand nine hundred and seventy-two cubic yards of masonry, and two hundred and forty-two thousand four hundred and nineteen feet board measure of timber-work; and the largest of the dams being of the height of fifty-eight feet, and the width one hundred and ninety feet, at the combing. In ascending this division of the Lehigh the commissioners passed through a succession of the largest and best-constructed and most easily-managed locks within their knowledge, and of such magnitude as greatly to exceed every public work in the United States. They were filled with admiration and delight as they examined these stupendous works, erected on that river which three years ago was wild, shallow, and useless, and has now been converted into a calm and beautiful stream, suited for all purposes of navigation, either for trade or pleasure, and will, as it is hoped and contemplated, be at no distant day navigated by sea vessels so constructed as to load at White Haven and discharge at ports along the Atlantic shore. The locks on the whole of the said navigation are of a capacity to pass boats of from one hundred and twenty to one hundred and fifty tons burden. The company having now fully complied with the law, and in a manner honorable to themselves, and (as Pennsylvanians we say with pride) most honorable to the State, we deem them entitled to a license for charging and collecting the legal toll."

The original plan in the minds of the originators of the works was to connect their navigation at White Haven on the Lehigh by canal, with the Susquehanna River at Berwick, along the valley of Nescopeck Creek, and by railroad with Wilkesbarre, on the same river, and in the centre of the third coal basin in the Wyoming

Valley. A canal to connect the Susquehanna and Lehigh rivers had been projected by other parties, and an act of the Assembly of Pennsylvania procured in 1826 for the purpose. Moncure Robinson, civil engineer, in 1828 had surveyed the route for the Canal Commissioners of the State, and made an estimate of the cost, and he reported that "no route between the rivers presents facilities for the construction of a canal deserving of consideration, except the Nescopeck route. But the whole fall to be overcome both ways is one thousand and thirty-eight feet," and "the most formidable obstacle in the way of the canal is unquestionably the lockage." The law was revived in 1834, and the route was again surveyed and estimates made by E. A. Douglas in 1836, and efforts made to induce the public to take the stock; but the idea was eventually abandoned, from the scarcity of water and other difficulties attending it.

In 1837 it was determined by the company to proceed with the construction of the railroad, and it was put under contract the same year, after a very thorough examination of the country by the engineer, E. A. Douglas, for several months, in order to ascertain the best location for it through the very rough and mountainous country over which it was to pass between the two rivers. To build this road required some very bold engineering, including a tunnel one thousand seven hundred and forty-three feet in length, and three inclined planes from the top of the mountain down through "Solomon's Gap" into the valley of the Susquehanna River. These planes were three in number, very substantially built, upon which the coal cars, by means of powerful stationary engines, were drawn out of the valley; from thence they were to be taken over the railroad to the head of the navigation on the Lehigh, twenty miles, and there shipped into boats on the canal. The height the coal was raised is about one thousand feet, and the planes were, respectively, four thousand eight hundred and ninety-four and twenty-four-one-hundredths feet, three thousand seven hundred and seventy-five and twenty-one-hundredths feet, and four thousand three hundred and sixty-one and twenty-eight-one-hundredths feet, in length; in the first the grade was about five feet, the second eight and six-tenths feet, and the third nine feet, in the hundred.

This road, and its tunnel of nearly one-third of a mile in length, the planes and heavy machinery, etc., were finally completed and put into use, after some delay in consequence of the damage to the canal by the freshet of 1841, and answered all the purposes intended, and a large amount of coal has been annually transported over it since. It was a work unprecedented in the United States at that time.

Another bold piece of engineering was also accomplished in 1845,—that of making a continuous and separate railroad to convey the empty coal cars back from Mauch Chunk to the mines.

For this purpose two powerful steam-engines of one hundred and twenty horse-power were placed on the eastern end of the mountain bounding the coal basin, about nine hundred feet above the Lehigh River at Mauch Chunk. From the head of the coal chutes the empty wagons are conveyed to the base of the mountain, and raised six hundred and sixty-five feet up an inclined plane of two tracks, two thousand three hundred and twenty feet in length, to its top; from thence they run down towards the mines, on a railroad of an average grade of fifty feet to the mile, six miles, to the foot of Mount Jefferson, and descending in this distance about three hundred feet; from this point they are again raised four hundred and sixty feet, upon a plane two thousand and fifty feet long, and thence by gravity a mile, to the town of Summit Hill, and down the Switch-Back Road into the valley of the Panther Creek, where the coal is mined and loaded. The loaded wagons, raised out of the valley by steam to Summit Hill, thence descend down the gravity road to Mauch Chunk for shipment. The cars are drawn up the planes with an iron strap or band attached to a drum about twenty-five feet in diameter, around the circumference of which it is wound by the power of the engine, bringing the cars up with it. The engines are so geared together that as the band on one track is wound up the other band descends, and *vice versa;* or they can be worked separately. The time of the ascent is from five to eight or ten minutes. Each band consists of two straps of four or five inches wide, one-eighth of an inch in thickness, placed alongside of each other, and fastened by short cross-pieces of the same size riveted on each at the joints, thus connecting them together. This Mount Pisgah plane was considered at the time of its construction the highest elevation overcome in this way in the world. The other plane at Mount Jefferson is worked on the same principle. The return track connects at Summit Hill, with the old gravity road from the mines to Mauch Chunk, thus making a continuous run by gravity (after the ascents are made) to the mines and back. This plan of the gravity road, over the mountains back to the mines, was the original idea of Josiah White, long before it was carried into successful operation, and frequently spoken of as desirable; it was made as soon as the trade would warrant the outlay.

In the year 1841, within less than three years after the completion of the upper section of the navigation, a disastrous freshet occurred on the Lehigh, whereby the works were greatly damaged. The upper section, from Mauch Chunk to Rockport, nine miles, was very badly injured; in some places almost totally destroyed. The river rose to an unprecedented height, in consequence of heavy rains and melted snow; the abutments of the dams were washed out, with many of the locks also, together with the canal, most of the high dams remaining intact.

Full of solicitude in regard to the event, Josiah White repaired to the scene of the devastation to ascertain the extent of the damage, and what would be required to repair it. He says in reference to it: "Perhaps the greatest personal exposure I ever underwent was in a few days after hearing of the sweeping flood on the Lehigh, I being then sixty years of age less about two months, though in good health. I had lived in the city for about nine or ten years, and experienced but little bodily exercise during this time, together with age having stiffened my muscles. The exercise I had, on going *on foot* up the banks of the canal to examine the inroads of the flood, with E. A. Douglas, our engineer, in snow and slush about six to nine inches deep, from South Easton to the Lehigh Gap, a distance of thirty-four miles, in *two days*, nearly exhausted me."

The company immediately went to work, and after some difficulties in financial and other matters, repaired and greatly strengthened the canal in less than two years.

It will thus be seen, that Josiah White was the leading spirit and designer of those stupendous enterprises connected with the works of the Lehigh Coal and Navigation Company, commencing with the very start of the project, to its final accomplishment, in which he was ably assisted by his coadjutor and friend Erskine Hazard. In addition to the construction of the cardinal parts of their undertaking there was a vast amount of minor details, involving and demanding as much ingenuity and patience to carry through as the larger works required, and upon which the success of the project in a measure depended.

CHAPTER VII.

MANUFACTURE OF ANTHRACITE IRON.

THE production of iron, by the use of anthracite coal, within the last thirty years, has become one of the leading industrial operations of Pennsylvania, and has enabled the State, at the present time, to be the largest producer of that metal in the United States, and its magnitude and importance are annually increasing.

The attention of Josiah White and Erskine Hazard had been early directed to the abundance of iron ore in the valley of the Lehigh and its neighborhood, and to the proximity of the two minerals, iron and coal; and the idea naturally arose in their practical minds of making them subservient to each other in the manufacture of iron. The Lehigh Coal and Navigation Company, also, had early become impressed with the importance of this manufacture to the interests of the coal trade, and at various times, as early as 1834, offered advantages to any company that would undertake it, by grants of water-power,—coal at reduced rates, and its transportation on the navigation, toll free to a large extent,—"provided they should succeed in introducing the business on the Lehigh."

Their report for 1838 says: "The long-agitated question of Pennsylvania anthracite coal being adapted, as a substitute for charcoal or coke, to the purpose of smelting iron ore, appears now to be fully established by our enterprising citizens, Messrs. Guiteau, Baughman, High & Lowthorp, who have a furnace at Mauch Chunk, which is now, and has been for thirty-two days continuously, free from all interruption, in full blast, exclusively with anthracite coal from our mines, and although a very small furnace, yields on an average one and a half tons a day. Their iron is believed to be of first quality, both as pig metal and for making bar iron. We view this success (which, however, we never doubted since the hot blast has been in use) as an earnest of much benefit to our company, to individuals who are, or may be, engaged in the iron business, and to the State at large."

These parties failed, eventually, to make the business successful, mainly from the furnace not being adapted to the purpose, and from defective hot-blast apparatus. These experiments, however, with those of Kunzie at Manayunk, Lyman at Pottsville, and Chambers at Danville, and its practical success in Wales, induced Josiah White, Erskine Hazard, and Thomas Earp, three of the then managers of the Lehigh Coal and Navigation Company, with others associated with them, to undertake the manufacture. This determination was come to, from much reliable and valuable information on the subject obtained from Josiah White's nephew, Solomon W. Roberts, who resided in Wales for several months, in 1837, and had investigated the whole subject. There he became acquainted with the inventor, George Crane, and was very favorably impressed with the practicability and importance of the process which he had discovered.

They and their associates in the undertaking became incorporated in 5th mo. 20, 1839, under the general law of Pennsylvania, for the manufacture of iron from coke or mineral coal, as "The Lehigh Crane Iron Company," with a capital of one hundred thousand dollars. The original stockholders, beside those mentioned, were Robert Earp, George Earp, John McAllister, Nathan Trotter, and Theodore Mitchell.

In 1838 Erskine Hazard went to Wales, and there made himself acquainted with the process and manner of making the anthracite iron; with the machinery and buildings needful for its manufacture. He ordered such machinery as was necessary to be made for the company,—under the direction of George Crane, the inventor,—and engaged David Thomas, who was familiar with the process, to take charge of the erection of the works and the manufacture of the iron. He arrived in the summer of 1839; and to his faithful and intelligent management much of the success of the enterprise is due.

The works were located at Catasaqua, on the Lehigh, about three miles above Allentown. Such has been the prosperity of the undertaking, that the company has six furnaces in operation at the present time, which produce a large amount of iron annually, the production for 1872 being fifty-four thousand tons.* A large town has grown up around them, having a population of five or six thousand people, mainly dependent for employment upon the prosperity of the iron business. The first boat-load of iron from their works shipped to Philadelphia arrived in August, 1840, about six weeks after the furnace was put in blast; on which the *North American*, of that city, remarks: "It is the opinion of those best qualified to judge in relation to such matters, that the new application of the anthracite, with which our mountains

* The present production of anthracite iron in the Lehigh valley, without any precise statistics to rely on, may be stated approximately to be, from forty furnace stacks, three hundred and twenty-five thousand tons per annum, which, at the present price of iron, is worth over thirteen millions of dollars; consuming, in its manufacture, six hundred and fifty thousand tons of coal, and eight hundred thousand tons of iron ore.

abound, forms an era in the history of Pennsylvania of which it would be difficult to over-estimate the importance. We may add that this conviction is gaining strength with every new trial of this mode of smelting iron."

Governor Porter, in his message to the legislature in 1840, referring to the subject, seemed to fully realize the great importance to the State of this process, when he says: "The value of coal and iron must necessarily be much enhanced by the recent successful application of anthracite coal as fuel for smelting iron ore, which will in all probability introduce a new era in the iron business in our Commonwealth. Possessing, as Pennsylvania does, the great bulk of the iron ore, and the anthracite coal formation of this country, in alternate strata in the same territory, and situated in a quarter of the Union peculiarly accessible by means of her geographical position, and canals and railroads, she must enjoy almost exclusively the great revenue that must arise from this source."

It will be difficult in the present day, to find in the United States any region of country where industrial operations are carried on to a greater extent, than in the valley of the Lehigh River, including the coal regions and its tributaries. When we take into view the immense proportions of its coal trade, largely supplying not only our own wants, but those of New York, New England, etc.; its mining, manufacture, and transportation to market, employing for that purpose a canal and two railroads, all first class of their kind; the mining of the ore, and the manufacture of iron in its various forms, not only pig, but bar, sheet, and railroad iron, etc.; and numerous other enterprises, connected with, or more or less dependent thereon; we may indeed be struck with surprise upon reverting to the past, to the rudiments of these things, only commenced about fifty years ago, and see to what in that time they have grown. And in looking forward, who can say, judging from the past, what is to be expected in the fifty years to come? That this valley is destined to be the richest, the most enterprising, and industrious, supporting as teeming and intelligent a population as any part of the United States, cannot, we think, be doubted. If its infancy has shown such robust proportions, what may be expected of its maturity?

All this prosperity has grown out of the ingenuity, enterprise, and indefatigable exertions of a few marked men. Men of foresight and energy, with but little capital in the beginning to carry out their plans; such men as Josiah White, Erskine Hazard, Judge Asa Packer, and a host of others, who came in later in the day, and who have put their energies to work to make this valley what it is, and to insure its prosperity in the future.

CHAPTER VIII.

RELIGIOUS EXERCISES.

IN advancing life Josiah White endeavored to loosen his mind from earthly care, and diligently to engage in the search after durable riches and righteousness. To give a faithful portraiture of his character, it is deemed needful to introduce some extracts from his copious reflections and private memoranda, the devotional exercises of his heart. These evince the simplicity and spirituality of his faith, and the earnestness of his piety.

"*8th month* 9, 1840.—O Lord Jesus, permit me, at least, to lay at thy feet, until Thou findest me devoted enough to lean on thy bosom. O Lord, if I realize no feeling but to have the eye of my mind turned towards Thee to the exclusion of every other thought or feeling, oh, permit me, if it please Thee, to enjoy this, therein humbly waiting thy time to break in upon me with the renewings of thy good presence. O Lord, strengthen my soul in Thee, so that nothing in this world interfere or resist its safe anchorage in Thee; then, indeed, is thy good presence felt as the stay and staff of my soul." Afterwards follow thanks for a religious meeting. "O Lord my God, permit me, and strengthen me, to bless thy holy name, and thank Thee, for in measure answering my preceding petition, for I now feel that it was not by might, or by my power, that in this afternoon meeting I was able to separate self and the world in a good measure from my meditation, resting in a small and thankful measure on thy goodness." Early in the following autumn he petitions thus: "O thou supreme Object of the soul's desire, oh, strengthen me, oh, support me, under all circumstances that Thou causest me, in thy inscrutable wisdom, to pass through, to hold on Thee; to be stayed on Thee, as the only rock of safety, as the only balm that heals, as the brook by the way, as the well of water bubbling up to eternal life, to eternal life in Thee."

12th mo. 22, 1840.—In his acknowledgment of near access to his heavenly Father, he writes: "Thou hast also permitted thy servant to know further, and to feel his poor soul being, at times, stayed on Thee, so as to perceptibly feel Thee. Instill in me more and more, I humbly beseech Thee, this feeling, which is far more nourishing, strengthening, and delightful than any, or even all, the aggregate pleasures of sense."

"*1st mo.* 1, 1841.—How solemn and grand is the entering into the Holy of Holies, and there to feel the sensible presence of the great God! O my soul, that thou wouldst never cease to press forward to attain as much of this state of feeling and enjoyment as thy God permits. Then would the divine cloud rest over the tabernacle door of my heart, and I should be still or move at its bidding through my wilderness journey of time. Then would my state be happy and my path sure. Oh, that my Lord of glory would fill me with insatiable desires to covet this way and path, above all things, for the remaining hours of my pilgrimage! Then could I indeed say, 'Tremble, thou earth, at the presence of the Lord, at the presence of the God of Jacob.'" (Psalm cxiv. 7.)

1st mo. 10, 1841.—On receiving the account of the disastrous flood on the Lehigh River of the 7th and 8th of that month, he petitions thus: "O Lord, help me to feel, as it in very deed is the truth, that all worketh together for good that cometh from thy unerring hand, and this affliction I know is from thy hand. Oh, let me beg of Thee to permit this apparent misfortune to drive me more close to Thee as the only rock of safety, as the only sure abiding-place against all storms and all disappointments; and above all things to seek peace in Thee; for it is in Thee alone all true and availing peace is to be found, both in time and eternity."

"*3d mo.* 28, 1842.—O Lord my God, permit me to bless thy holy name; to thank Thee for thy continued remembrance of thy servant, for not dealing with him according to his deserts, but according to thy tender mercies. Thou, Lord, my Father, hast pitied me in making me in measure to feel how weak I am, and how depending on Thee for every ray of good, lest I should despair. Thou hast, in thy loving kindness, made me feel thy goodness to overshadow me yesterday, in afternoon meeting. Oh, that this sense might be more often felt, so that I might live nearer and nearer to Thee! Then could I say in truth, The Lord liveth! the Lord is known among his people!"

Of the Passover, he wrote: "The Paschal Lamb was first offered at the great epoch of the delivery of the Israelites from bondage, and was kept annually as a memorial of that great event. The offering and the delivery from bondage were strictly of a temporal character, and applied only to temporal circumstances, but at the same time typical of the offering of our Redeemer for the saving of the soul of man,—not of Israel only but of the whole human family. Nothing of a temporal nature was intended by the last offering: it was all for a spiritual object."

* * * * * * *

"*8th mo.* 24, 1843.—'At the name of Jesus every knee shall bow.' This great and glorious name passed through my mind this morning in an involuntary manner, and produced a solemn and placid feeling, entirely unattainable by any effort of mine. Like a passing meteor in the sky, bright, and moving in majesty, and directed by the great Architect himself, entirely free from all the agency of man, even so passed the holy name of Jesus with power and calm pleasantness indescribable through my mind. I sought to keep the impression, but it passed from me. O Lord Jesus, may I beseech Thee to make thy visits nearer and nearer to each other, until I can keep hold on Thee as my best beloved. What, O Lord, is so lovely?"

"*1st mo.* 17, 1844.—The name of Jesus was sweet to my soul early this morning, and before I got up from my bed, and so continues. O Lord my God, wilt Thou condescend to keep this sweetness in my mind,—for Thou only, and not myself, art able to do so.

"O Lord Jesus, may I humbly adore Thee for thy goodness, in making thy sweet abode with me this morning. Oh, help me to hold Thee fast, and to keep near Thee during the remainder of this life, so that when my days of probation are over, I may land in thy everlasting mansions, and there join thy redeemed, in thy praise forever."

"*1st mo.* 18.—O Lord Jesus, why hast Thou left me? Why hast Thou gone by and left me, poor and helpless as I am when left to myself, and cannot find Thee? Is it to teach me my wants and my poverty without Thee, and that Thou visitest me at thy pleasure, and not at mine?—for wisdom is thine only, and Thou only knowest the best time. Oh, how barren my feelings in thy absence! How lamentably poor am I, thy servant, when Thou leavest me!—not a single ray of good seems to be my portion; nothing to say but to lament my coldness and my barrenness when Thou, my love, my endeared One, art not to be found by me. O Lord, may it please Thee not to stay from me long, but return and abide with me, for thy lovely presence is felt to be sweeter than honey, and more pleasant to me and more desirable than all else beside. When Thou art felt to be present all thy creation smiles on me, for with Thee is the fruition of all that is harmonious and good. Thy love is pure, and binds all thy devoted children as one man in the love of each other, and in the love of Thee above all."

* * * * * * *

"*5th mo.* 1.—Christ is declared to be the desire of all nations. To realize in our hearts this Divine Being of love and power, casts all other feelings and desires in the shade. It is even He that said, 'I will not leave you comfortless; I will come to you;' and 'without Me ye can do nothing;' and 'where two or three are gathered together in my name, there am I in the midst.'"

"*9th mo.* 22.—O Lord my God, permit me, if it

pleaseth Thee, to thank Thee for strengthening me, for, in a small measure, feeling Thee in yesterday afternoon meeting. Small as it was, it renewed my hope that I might yet again feel and know Thee in truth, and that as Thou livest I shall live also."

"*3d mo.* 4, 1845.—My birthday; age 64. O Lord, here am I, thy servant, fast severing the cord of this life, and settling down to that period wherein time to me shall be no more. Oh, may I beg of Thee to aid me to keep my account and interest in Thee, and look to Thee as my only hope, and as my sure friend; then let my end come whenever Thou markest the time, I know it will be peace; for because Thou livest I shall live also, for Thou always standest by the man whose only trust is in Thee.

"O Lord God, may I beg of Thee to touch the hearts of my beloved wife and children and domestics, and all my fellow-men, with myself, with the touches of thy parental love, so as to woo and entice us all to thy fold, that our end may be peace, everlasting peace in Thee."

* * * * * * *

"*5th mo.* 22.—This was our week-day meeting, and a day ever to be remembered, as, early after I sat down, I was favored to feel a little light in my heart. On it my mind was turned, and favored to rest with very little interruption during the whole meeting. I felt I could continue there a long while, in the enjoyment of heavenly peace. I in very deed believe it was the light of Christ in me, as He promised to be my hope of glory if I could keep close to Him as my guide.

"*5th mo.* 23.—Jesus has left me; that sweetness and peace which covered my mind yesterday, and, until I went to sleep, at my usual time last night. I awoke at night and found my guide had left me, and this morning his goodness is still hid from me.

"O Lord, what barrenness when Thou art gone! what leanness of spirit when Thou hast left me! I feel void of the sense of good when thy face is hidden from me, so that I cannot realize thy sweetness; I can do nothing but mourn until thy return."

* * * * * *

"*6th mo.* 1, 1846.—In yesterday afternoon meeting I was favored by a higher power than my own, to keep my mind, nearly through the whole meeting, on the light of Christ, to the exclusion of nearly all other thoughts; for some hours after, I felt a peace and comfort that nothing of this world can give."

In the summer of 1846, being absent from home, in a letter to his daughters, he shows his parental interest and solicitude thus:

"Most truly the heart would be lost to gratitude that did not love and adore the hand by which it is fed. It is our heavenly Father that feeds us with every item of our nourishment, and gives to each crumb its appropriate direction, whether it be to sicken or to heal; and, under either allotment, it is our place to give Him thanks, as He is equally our care-taker in sickness and in health.

"You are still in the morning of your days, with the promise of all the blessings of this world's abundance before you. What if He that gives you these blessings should be pleased to say, great as these are, I have stores far transcending in the world above, waiting for you?

"Be assured, all that is of the other world will, if resorted to, yield its power and its consolation. Therefore, in all our troubles, our true consolation is not found here, but in the heavens above; in Him who lived and died for our salvation."

"*6th mo.* 12, 1847.—O my soul, do thou reflect on the goodness of thy Redeemer, who has promised to come in to thee, and to sup with thee, and permit thee to sup with Him."

"*8th mo.* 9.—Oh, what a good paymaster is my Lord!—when He makes himself known to me all within me rejoices."

"10*th mo.* 13.—'The peace of God.' This universal peace and love expands the soul illimitably, beyond the thoughts and imaginations of all things of a mundane character, and raises it within itself to a heavenly union with its Author, thus causing it to partake of angels' food. For some considerable time past my mind has had no rest, and without participating in any sense of this peace I have been seeking for, and nothing within me seemed to help me, all was dry and barren. This morning, soon after awaking, without efforts of self, this divine peace in a small measure broke in upon my soul, and plainly showed me that my only hope of enjoying it was in seeking divine aid, to prostrate all self-will, and rest the soul entirely and exclusively on the divine will."

"*8th mo.* 8, 1848.—'God is love.' The subject of this love engaged my attention this morning before I arose, and as my mind was directed to the various branches of it, a small grain of its leaven seemed to leaven it, and gave me a little sweetness."

"*8th mo.* 13.—'Christ in you the hope of glory.' These words ran through my mind this morning, in meeting, much to my edification, as I was favored to plainly see the *vast difference* between a *feeling* of Christ in me, as the hope of glory, and living under his direct influence in my heart; than to *talk*, and *reason*, or *read* of Christ within, the hope of glory. The former being the possession of Christ, and the latter the hearsay of Him."

* * * * * * *

"10*th mo.* 17.—O Lord my Father, how shall I declare praises, yes, everlasting praises, to thy holy name, for keeping with me this afternoon in my effort of devotion, and finding peace with Thee?

"O Lord my God my Saviour, what a favor it is to have felt thy light with me all this time, so that I have experienced a small glimpse of Thee!

"O my Lord, strengthen me, if it please Thee, to love industry,—the industry that seeketh after Thee,—and strive to gain Thee above all things; yea, never feel satisfied until I find Thee, and feel my love and my peace alone in Thee.

"Well, indeed, did George Fox and his friends hold up to the world Christ as the light within man, as his guide, director and only hope; not from hearsay or study of books, but from experimentally feeling and knowing Him. This, of calling Christ the light, was not new to either covenant." Psalm xxvii. 1; John i. 4.

11*th mo.* 9, 1848.—"O Lord, may I throw my case before Thee, and place myself under thy divine care and admonition, and seek thy wisdom and thine alone, to guide me in my great strait at this time.

"Oh, that I may in *all* my straits look unto Thee for thy divine help, and in thy help abide, as the fountain and source of all that is right and proper, so seeketh, so prayeth, thy servant, and worm of the dust, at this time, and giveth to Thee all the glory and the praise both now and forever."

"3*d mo.* 5, 1849.—Yesterday was my sixty-eighth birthday. The awfulness of the scene ahead is, indeed, enough to call for all the industry and energy of the soul, of every one, in his appeals to, and devotion to God's appointed Saviour for man, to have *mercy* and *spare* for lukewarmness and direct disregard of Him.

"O Lord, aid me to bury all acts and all thoughts, that are in the way of my finding Thee, so that I may make sure of Thee at last. Oh, may it please Thee to be also with my beloved wife and family, and wean us all from this world, and centre each of our minds in Thee, whose glories shine in the world of spirits, free from all veils; where we all one day may hope to meet, with praises, everlasting praises, to Thee, O Lord God, our heavenly Father, and Jesus Christ, my Saviour."

11*th mo.* 5, 1849.—On going to Mount Holly, to attend the funeral of a cousin, he visited many places in and near this town, fraught with interesting early reminiscences. Part of his business appears to have been to look after a site for a free school, remarking: "I thought I had offered enough for my partiality to the old estate," etc.

"About 8 A.M. started for the old church-ground; passed by the corner of the fence and graveyard where, some sixty years since, I dreamed seeing my heavenly Father, and He spoke so comfortably to me, that I feel a sense of the comfort down to this day. Here I paid Him my devotions for the pilgrimage in which He had so long led and preserved me.*

"I afterwards proceeded to our meeting-house on Button Street, hoping that when there I might feel some sense of whether my views at Mount Holly, in relation to a free school, were correct or not; for in this thing my prayers have long been, that He who said 'without Me ye can do nothing,' would, in feeling, clearly manifest to me his approval, or otherwise; for in the pursuit of this I hope I have no other object in view but that of being instrumental, in his hands, of bringing souls to his kingdom."

* * * * * *

REFLECTIONS.

"*11th mo.* 23.—When I consider the relationship of man to his Maker, how depending he is before Him, yea, nothing but a clod of dust, and the life he lives is only by the will and power of the Holy One, it is even He, that created this dust, and gave it life, and being, and capacity, to serve Him, and do his will, and to live forever!

---

* The previous fall, in a visit to the same locality, he records: "Here, on my bended knees, I poured out my prayer to my heavenly Father for the preservation of myself and my beloved family during the remainder of our pilgrimage in this life of probation, and, finally, to take us one and all to Himself."

"If man presents himself before his fellow-man, of a princely station in life, how silent and respectful is he before him, and waiting until his king speaks, and gives authority to him to reply or to say aught!

"How much more respectful and reverential should this child of the dust appear before his Maker and heavenly Father! how cheerful and how patient should he be in his waiting and watching for the coming of his divine presence in his soul!

"Ah! how unspeakably awful it is to feel this divine presence near us, for '*nothing*' to have a sense and consciousness of Him that is '*everything*'! Oh how awful, how calculated to still the boisterous wave, and to say to all the motions of time and sense, Be still before Me, the Creator and Sustainer of all things! Such a Being will surely not accept a part or portion of thine heart; thou must give it all to Him or none.

"But where shall I go to find Him whom my soul seeks above all things, however attractive the things of time and sense are, that habit has made so natural to me? Yet, when I contemplate, how transient, how nothing, are all these, in comparison to the promises of eternity, to a being who has an immortal soul, how little, how nothing, are all these things of time and sense in the contrast!

"Surely, I need not seek Him in the hills, valleys, or plains of this world, or in the wonderful and unnumbered worlds made and arranged by Him in the concave above; in no place will I find Him but where He promised to be, saying, 'He that is with you shall be in *you*.' Thy Father and thy Lord comes here to thee, when thou hast prepared the ground of thy heart to receive Him; there prepare it by a quiet, unresisting submission to his holy will, and there look to and for his light, and wait for it, be the time long or short; be patient in thy seeking Him, and wait his time to break in on thee, for his only is the right time."

"12*th mo.* 31.—End of the year. When I look back over the past year, and reflect how many of my fellow-creatures of about my age have been called to the bourne from whence there is no return, and of the various incidents threatening to place me there, I am led to wonder why it is, my Maker and heavenly Parent has continued me yet a little longer; and, shall I hope and pray unto Him that for the time He may still extend to me a further existence in this his world of probation, that He will increase in me living desires every day to serve and love Him; and for the past preservation for myself and my family, may He beget in me and in them, heartfelt thankfulness therefor, and may this thankfulness be evinced by our increased desire to serve and to love Him, from whom all good and all preservation come."

"*3d mo.* 4, 1850.—My sixty-ninth birthday. My heavenly Parent having thus lengthened out my existence to this period of life, and brought me into that year which is called in Scripture the life of man (and if other years be added they are to be considered extraordinaries, rather than in the ordinary course of human nature), and thus has added to my days opportunities to serve, and thank Him therefor. Oh, how much am I indebted to my Lord for thus giving me time to prepare for eternity!—for He desires not the death of a sinner, but that all should repent, return to Him, and live.

"Oh, when I look over my past time, and perceive how much of it is lacking in devotion to my Lord, I am brought into a feeling of awe and awfulness. We need not blame others, not even Satan, our greatest enemy, for our lost time, for He that has all power will save us, if *the fault* is not ours."

"*8th mo.* 11, *First-day.*—I was permitted to keep my mind centred on the light of Christ in it, most of the meeting, and I thought I should have received it as a favor to have doubled the length of the meeting in the possession of this divine goodness, if it pleased Him to continue with me. When the meeting broke, and for hours afterwards, a glow of divine feeling continued with me, which was far greater and sweeter than any mundane thing."

* * * * * * *

"*8th mo.* 21.—'I in them, and Thou in Me.'

"Can anything be more clear and conclusive, that all our hopes of heaven and heavenly things are to be in Christ, and that we are to find Him in *no* earthly, no material thing, no show, no sound, and in naught, but in our own hearts? Yes, in the *silent* waiting and feeling of the heart, there we are to find Him; there, and there only, is to be our prostration; man is then to retire inward, in his own soul, and there to wait for, and to find his God and Saviour; there, he is to worship and adore Him; there, he is to lay at the feet of Jesus, and surrender to Him his whole will, and beg of Him to take his will from him, and make him a new creature, with his Lord's will only to exclusively direct him.

"This indeed is the state my soul longs for and covets above all things. Oh, that all my days, hours, and moments, that my God permits me to stay on earth, I may feel this desire to increase, so that when my end comes I shall be ready, and waiting for my Lord!"

CONCLUSION.

In the autumn of the year 1850 he made a journey to the West, as far as Richmond, Indiana, and attended the yearly meeting of the Society of Friends, held there at that time; going north, by the lakes; and returning through Cincinnati, and by the Ohio River, to Pittsburg, thence, by the Pennsylvania Canal, the Portage Railroad, Harrisburg and Lancaster, home. The journey was protracted and fatiguing, and he was not well on his arrival. He continued indisposed, hoping to be better after the wear of the journey was over: but this was not the case, and on the 6th of the 11th mo. the disease, which had been slowly developing, was pronounced by his physician to be remittent fever, contracted during his absence. It afterwards assumed a typhoid character, affecting the head; and his mind at times became much clouded and wandering, but he evinced much patience and calmness in his sickness. Not having put off the work of preparation to the last moment, he knew where to look for consolation in this time of need. Being seldom in a condition for much concentration of thought or religious introversion of mind, was a trial to him. It was requisite that he should be kept in a state of quietness, and free from excitement of any kind. On the 12th inst. a minister of the gospel visited him. She spoke to him of the comfort there is in looking upon the Almighty as our father, able to call Him by the endearing name of father, to which he assented. She remarked he had stood for the cause of truth and righteousness in the world, not being afraid to confess Christ before men, and she believed he would be blessed for it. He acknowledged, in great humility, he had nothing whereof to boast. Supplication was also offered, and the belief was expressed that he had not put off the work of preparation until this time. Next day, on reference being made to this kind call, he spoke touchingly of his mind not having been in a state to communicate much; and of a mind being so affected, as to be hardly able to realize things around it, there was so much feebleness in its grasp.

On being reminded that he had been a diligent reader of the Holy Scriptures, he replied "that that would not avail; but communion with Heaven, that was good." The progress of the disease continued without much intermission, notwithstanding the most assiduous care of his physicians and family, until he sank into a stupor, from which his imprisoned soul was released from its earthly tabernacle on the 14th of the 11th mo., 1850, in the seventieth year of his age.

"Blessed are the poor in spirit, for theirs is the kingdom of heaven."

In person Josiah White was rather below medium stature, inclining to corpulency in later life, his complexion clear and florid. He might be considered as the embodiment of the earnest, sanguine, and persevering, with a strong and persistent will, seldom calculating on failure in his undertakings. He had no patience with ostentation or false pretensions of any kind, but admired the practical and useful, making no display in his personal appearance or manner of living. To those unacquainted with him his manners may have appeared somewhat stern and his speech abrupt, and opinions decided; but he had the milk of human kindness in his heart, was tender in his feelings, ready to assist the needy and destitute, and those in trouble, without distinction of nation, color, or creed, by money, sympathy, or counsel. He possessed a cheerful, social disposition, being fond of the society of his friends, of whom he had a large number in different classes of society; was given to hospitality; but when he thought it his duty to rebuke error, either privately or publicly, though it might be in high places, he did it fearlessly and unflinchingly. His industry was a strong trait in his character, and even in latter years, when he had declined taking much active part in business, he generally kept himself employed in some useful occupation, either with his hands or pen, and despised idleness in any form whatever.

He had a remarkable faculty of strongly attaching to his person and interests those who were employed by him, gaining their confidence and respect by the interest he took in the prosperity of themselves and families; rejoicing at and promoting the success of those, who by their worth, industry, and talents, proved themselves entitled to his confidence and regard.

He was much interested in the subject of education, particularly desiring its diffusion among the lower classes of the people, in a way to make them self-reliant and self-supporting, often contributing liberally of his means for such purposes.

He bequeathed funds for the establishment of two manual labor schools in the West,—one in Indiana, the other in Iowa,—especially having reference to the religious training of the pupils.

Learning and accomplishments may excite admiration and praise; but the higher qualities of uniform Christian integrity of character and generous benevolence of heart can alone insure lasting respect and influence among our fellow-men.

APPENDICES.

LEVEL OF THE WATER WHEN THE LOCK IS FILLED
D
CHUTE
LONGITUDINAL SECTION
CRIBBING & MASONRY
CHAMBER
A
B
CRIBBING
D
C
E
10 FEET
CHUTE
17 FEET
ENTRANCE TO LOCK
CRIBBING
10 FEET

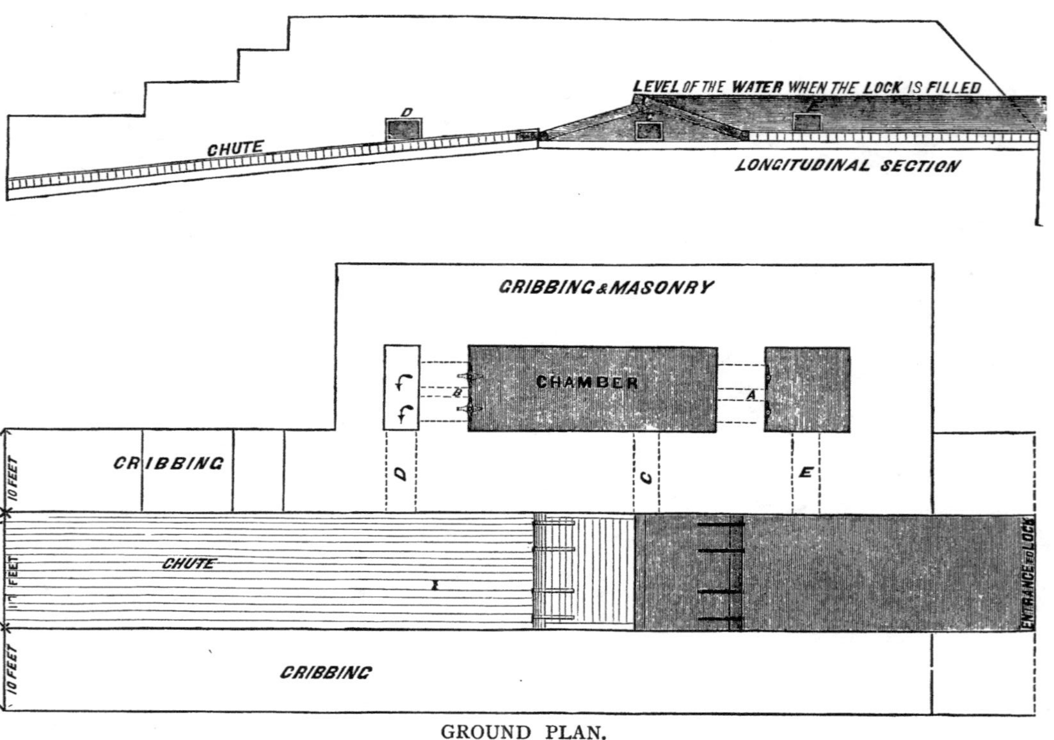

GROUND PLAN.

APPENDIX No. I.

EXPLANATION OF THE "BEAR-TRAP LOCK," SHOWN ON THE OPPOSITE PAGE.

THERE is a ground plan and longitudinal section figured. To fill the lock the wickets at B are closed, and those at A opened; the water then passes through the sluices E and A, into the large chamber, from whence it passes through the sluice, C, underneath the gates, and lifts them.

To empty the lock the wickets at A are closed, and those at B are opened. The water from the chamber and under the gates goes through the sluices B and D into the chute; the gates drop and the water passes over them and down the chute, carrying the boat with it.

These locks can be made of any capacity to suit the amount of water, the fall, and size of the boat intended to be used; though they are not suited to any very great descent. In the one shown, the chamber of the lock is fifty-six feet long to the apex of the gates, seventeen feet wide, with four and a half feet depth of water. The chute is sixty-eight feet long,—scale, twenty-five feet to an inch.

Three of these locks are still in use on the upper Lehigh, between White Haven and Stoddartsville.

APPENDIX No. 2.

DELAWARE NAVIGATION.

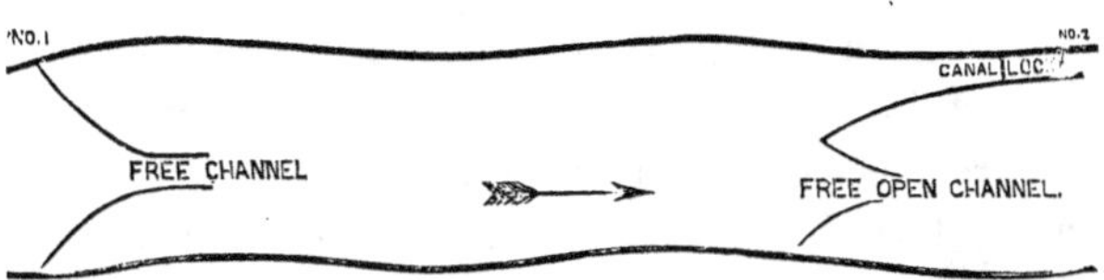

THE above is a sketch of the plan proposed for the improvement of the river Delaware, by the Lehigh Coal and Navigation Company.

No. 1 represents the kind of improvement to be adopted at all the falls where the water can be made three feet deep by means of wing dams (or by sinking the bottom of the river), to confine it in an open channel, without making it too rapid for a boat to ascend by the power of a steam-engine,—all such channels to be improved by the company and kept in repair at their expense, and to be used by the public *free of toll.*

No. 2 is an example of the improvement of a fall, where the water would be too rapid for the ascent of a steamboat by the power of her engines.

In all such cases, a lock, thirty feet wide and one hundred and thirty feet long, would be made at one of the shores, and all boats, etc., *using the lock*, either in ascending or descending, would be subject to toll. But at these places the present channels would be left uninterrupted and free for the passage of boats without toll. The work to be conducted in such a manner that the use of the river by boats and rafts, on the present plan, shall not be interrupted during any stage of its progress. Openings can be left in the wings near the shore to admit the upward passage of the Durham boats.

NOTE.—The above plan guarantees the continuance forever of a free open channel, improved and kept in repair at the expense of the company, except the channels in the same fall with the lock, which will be left open as they now are. It also guarantees forever against any obstructions to the usual running of the fish up the river. No part of the improvement overflows or injures private property. The mills at present erected on the river will be secured in their titles, and finally, the river will be made capable of transporting a greater amount of tonnage than any canal now in existence.

From the inspection of the map of Pennsylvania, it will be evident that the improvement of the Delaware must be a matter of deep interest to nearly one-half of the population of this State and of New York, as canals to connect it with the

Susquehanna and with the New York Grand Canal at the Seneca River are quite practicable, and this route would have the advantage of being the shortest, and of affording, upon arrival at Easton, the choice of the two best markets in the country, —that of Philadelphia, by the Delaware, and that of New York, by the Jersey Canal.

The Lehigh Coal and Navigation Company have proposed this plan, and are desirous it should be adopted, either by the State on its own account, or by the borough of Easton, or by a new incorporation; or if none of these are willing to undertake the task, they ask the liberty of doing it themselves. If the State would undertake it, and make the *locks free*, the Lehigh Company would contribute handsomely to the work.

APPENDIX No. 3.

TABLE.

Showing the Production of Coal at the Lehigh Coal and Navigation Company's Mines in the first coal region, since their origin. From Official Reports.

YEAR.	TONS.
1820	365
1821	1,073
1822	2,440
1823	5,823
1824	9,541
1825	28,393
1826	31,280
1827	27,770
1828	33,150
1829	25,110
1830	43,000
1831	44,500
1832	77,292
1833	124,508
1834	106,500
1835	131,250
1836	146,738
1837	200,000
1838	154,693
1839	142,507
1840	102,264

YEAR.	TONS.
1841	78,164
1842	163,762
1843	138,826
1844	219,245
1845	257,740
1846	284,813
1847	351,675
1848	360,619
1849	393,807
1850	424,258
1851	480,824
1852	510,406
1853	496,905
1854	544,811
1855	449,812
1856	400,425
1857	400,751
1858	425,896
1859	546,816
1860	517,157
1861	410,877
1862	241,837
1863	517,259
1864	517,180
1865	517,025
1866	400,000
1867	370,204
1868	467,126
1869	472,410
1870	297,471
1871	518,800
Total	13,705,298

www.ingramcontent.com/pod-product-compliance
Lightning Source LLC
LaVergne TN
LVHW021413110826
845150LV00007B/1907

* 9 7 8 1 4 2 5 5 1 0 1 9 0 *